Unpolished Journey:
An uncensored look at recovery from an eating disorder

Morgan Blair

Published by Eliezer Tristan Publishing
Portland, OR

Copyright © 2019 by Morgan Blair

Illustrations by Alice Gothberg
Cover design by Aaron Smith

Dedicated to all those still fighting, those who no longer can, and those who have somehow found freedom from the darkness. Mental illness is real and this book is for you —if only, to feel a little less alone.

Unpolished Journey is a community I created back in 2016. I wanted a space where I could connect with others in recovery from mental illness. The community quickly grew into a group of creatives sharing their stories through art. Art being any form of expression - painting, drawing, yoga, dance, spoken word, etc. *Unpolished Journey* is a place where people are allowed to be raw, authentic, and express with boundaries, because of this, I have never felt more at home among a group of people.

Lately, I've been thinking about why I started *Unpolished Journey* in the first place. To be honest, it had more to do with a desire to share my story than it did to create a place for others to share their own. In 2016 when I made that first post on Instagram, all I really wanted was to meet people who understood the struggle, who could relate, who were going through something similar. Lo and behold, that happened. Of course that happened because everyone is going through, or has gone through, some kind of struggle. It was through the people I was meeting and the stories I was reading that I decided I wanted *Unpolished Journey* to be a space for everyone. Everyone struggling with mental illness would be welcome to have a space to share their story so that they may receive the same connection I did after I made that first post.

The community aspect of Unpolished has been so empowering and wonderful, but I feel like I have walked away from the platform of sharing my own story. So, I started digging through my old journals. The ones kept during hospital stays, treatment centers, and my own struggle of living with mental illness in the world. I call them my recovery diaries as they document a desire to get better while showing the true ups and downs towards finding freedom.

Through the recovery diaries, I wanted to give people a glimpse into what a day in recovery from an eating disorder, PTSD, and depression truly looks like. I want people to be able to connect and feel less alone because, let's face it, recovery is not perfect and we all deserve to be reminded of that.

Disclaimer: The following entries are raw and unedited. Please, pause to evaluate your own journey and where your tolerance level for reading about another's explicit struggle lies. Do what's best for you. I know when I was deep in my illnesses, I read many memoirs that left me triggered and uncomfortable. There is nothing wrong with putting this book down and deciding that it is not appropriate to read at this time.

Write hard and clear about what hurts.

2013: the first admittance of needing help, the first diagnosis, the first therapist, the first time I saw there were others, others who struggle just like me, the few journal entries that weren't torn and left in a pile of tears

07/23/13

Love is hard to understand.

* * *

08/17/13

The future: what a terrifying topic for someone who has no idea where to go.

* * *

09/13/13

I wrestle constantly between the lies of this world and the lies of myself.

* * *

12/28/13

A mantra for the New Year:

I am not inferior to anyone.

I have the power within me to make every day the best day of my life.

2014: *a failure to admit to how deep the struggle was becoming, a health decline, a sense of fear, and an eventual realization that recovery must get worse before it gets better.*

02/20/14

One, two, three, running, no crawling, lying flat on the
ground, I smell the pavement, I look up, someone, anyone, I
reach out…

Crawling, crawling, crawling, cuts on my knees—*it's baby
steps*- words whisper through the air, dissolving in the wind,
I feel them fly past, nothing helps…

nothing sticks.

02/21/14

I wish I could just continue the way I had been living. So what if food ruled my life? At least it brought me comfort. It was so much simpler. They tell me I can't continue this way because I will die. Not mentally, not emotionally, but literally. I don't want to die. Not yet. I just want everything to be easier, to feel lighter. Why can't I have an eating disorder and a life? I want both.

I crave both.

02/24/14

When pain comes, imagine yourself in quicksand. Just stand there, feel the pain for what it is, because if you try to fight it, you sink lower. You begin to create, for yourself, your own suffering.

02/27/14

I am hiding my face from the world around me. My eyes are fixed downward and my shoulders hunched. My mouth must remain shut. I can't be accepted with all this baggage. I can't have someone care in this battle because I am a failing warrior, fighting with little strength. My efforts seem small—a snack here, a meal there. To those outside it is all insignificant. All I can wish now is to become air and blow away wherever the wind may take me. But, to return to the stage where I lack any care would mean I surrender to defeat. I can't, but fighting seems to leave me lost and pain stricken. No one should accept this conflicted person I have become. Please, allow me to first morph into something beautiful...if only...if only. But, addictions are ugly, pain is sticky, and disorders are messy.

I want people to run from my shame, to turn their backs on my torn and raging self. I want them to run away quickly before they, too, become encapsulated by this inescapable darkness. Please, let them hear me now. *Just run as fast as you possibly can.*

I know this disease, this anorexic parasite inside my mind, is my enemy. It's controlling and manipulative and full of empty promises that only leave me isolated and suffocated in darkness. It takes over and shields me from any chance of love and acceptance. I know all this, and yet I go back. I go back and listen to all its lies, as if it is my best friend giving me trusted advice. I buy the laxatives, I restrict for a day, I binge. I know I am slipping away, far, far away to a place where no light shines and only destruction prevails.

Anorexia is what true isolation looks like.

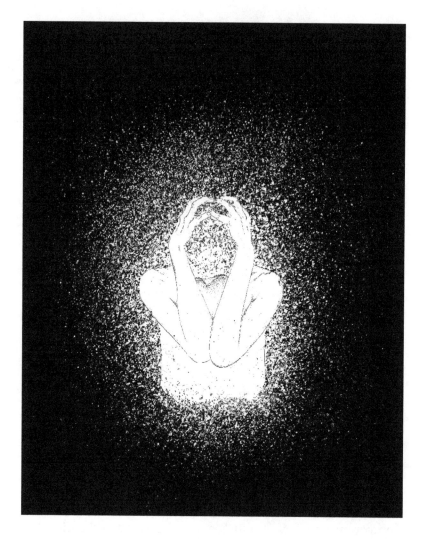

03/01/14

Up All Night.

I can't sleep. I can't think straight. My eating disorder is raging. It is loud. It is angry. It is brutal. And I am panicking. I can't sleep. My body seems to have grown thirty pounds in each passing hour.

03/2/14

I am not stupid. I know there is a war going on inside of me.
I know the parasite has clawed, scratched, and manipulated
my thoughts into believing I am worthless.

Why is it that it never crossed my mind that I could put on
armor to protect myself?

It is simply too hard to admit to needing a full body of armor
to get up and even face the day.

03/08/14

I am sick of surviving. I want to live.

03/09/14

How is it that at one moment, things can be so beautiful, seem so perfect, and feel so right and then the next, you are struck by complete darkness? How is it that at one moment, recovery seems within reach and the next, it is something I wish nothing to do with? How is it that my mind can switch from healthy to destruction so quickly, and with no remorse?

I am two different people: a slave to one and fighting for the other. Both are a part of me, both I cherish, both I love, and yet I know I must choose one or the other. No person can have two selves, right?

I know which one I should choose and, lately, I have chosen to be that healthy person. The person who wishes for recovery, who believes in its promise of a long and happy life, a person who knows a God that will help me get there. But last night, my other half came knocking at my door. At first I didn't answer. I turned my back, but she was persistent and my mind was weak. She stayed pounding, yelling, and demanding that I let her in.

Why are you working for recovery, Morgan? You know you don't want that. It's too hard. You're just going to get fat and feel awful about yourself. It's not worth it. You're not worth it. Come on, just open up. Let me in. You will feel so much better. You know me. You're comfortable around me. Just open up and let me in.

And what did I do when this person, this destructive being that I have worked so hard to distance myself from, kept calling? I listened, believed what she was yelling, opened the door, and let my other self take control.

From the moment I had done so, everything was distorted. My thoughts were instantly switched from the joy of the summer internship to how many calories the dessert was that I had just eaten in celebration. My thoughts pulled me out of the conversation I was having about life, the future, and friendship, and toward destructive behaviors. I could see it in my mind, the slippery slope that I was beginning to slide down.

Full of hundreds of calories of butter cake and utterly consumed in my destructive thoughts, I didn't talk much on the way back to the dorms. I blamed it on tiredness, but, in reality, I wasn't tired at all. My mind was racing, my armpits sweating, and my heart pounding. I knew I wasn't going to sleep tonight. Rather, I would engage in a party for two, me and my eating disorder. When I closed my dorm room door behind me and was certain I was alone, my destructive self immediately turned from thoughts to actions. So, commenced a wondrously entertaining night of binging, purging, and crying myself to sleep while thinking of how to compensate tomorrow for the food still sitting in my stomach.

And so I ask again, how is it that at one moment things can be so beautiful, seem so perfect, and feel so right, and then the next, you are struck by complete darkness? My day had been good, wonderful, in fact, but all of these good things were no match against my fighting, bullying, strong, and powerful eating disorder self. When she came, she wasn't leaving until all the good that I had experienced throughout the day was removed from my mind and she was all I was left with.

It is a destructive, dysfunctional relationship that I keep going back to. Just me and her. A party for two.

03/10/14

Would you ever look at a child and wish upon them the struggles you were dealing with? Would you take the burden you are carrying and hand it over to them?

Remember darling, never eat after 5pm.
Always be the last to finish.
Eat half of what's on your plate.
And, above all else, shrink. Yes, shrink with everything you've got.

03/12/14

Why is the shower not hot?

I turn the nozzle farther to the left.

> *Warm up!*

But it doesn't.

> > Farther.
> > > *Warm up!*

But it doesn't.

The luke-warm water continues to stream down my skin. Tears well in my eyes. My shoulders rise and fall. Uncontrollable sobs follow.

Stupid.
> It's all so stupid.
> > *This.*
> > > *That.*
> > > > *Which.*
> > > > > *Was.*

I don't know.

Why is the shower not hot?

03/16/14

It has been nine years. Nine years of dieting, hating myself, wishing I were thinner, sicker, prettier. Nine years wasted over petty worries like calories, exercising, body image. I don't remember much else. I remember what I ate. I remember the amount of calories I was consuming. I remember what my measurements were. I remember how much I weighed. But I don't remember anything else. Nine years wasted.

Why can't I leave that in the past? Why can't I get up and move forward? I saw it for a moment. Recovery. It looked so sweet, beautiful, but full of empty promises. Promises that my narcissistic mind couldn't believe. I saw it for a little while...but I don't see it anymore. All I see are numbers. Goals. Wishes. Thinner. Thinner. Thinner.

God, where are you? Where is your healing in all of this? I am slipping. Don't you care? I am slipping, God. Slipping quickly. I don't see a hand to grab on to. I don't see a release. I don't see a way out. Yes, I have slipped. Back down into the dark release of this disease. It's sadistic.

Oh, how I have missed the destructive safety it offers me. It tastes too alluring for me to turn away. So I don't. I continue on into a tunnel I know will never end.

03/24/14

What if I don't want to give up my disorder? What if I still want to lose weight? What if shrinking is all I cherish? What if I it's all I know to do?

I'm sorry if you can't understand.

03/28/14

I no longer want to obsess over my body. I no longer want to be a slave to my weight, calories, or my compulsive thoughts about food. I want more to life than throwing up, diet pills, and becoming a slave to the gym. I no longer want to feel worthless and broken. I want to meet the girl I was designed to be, if there is any of her left to meet.

* * *

04/03/14

I don't know who I am beyond my eating disorder. It has hypnotized me for so long.

04/07/14

truth is a strange magic
once spoken its power ceases
but never uttered and it gains power every moment
truth is a strange magic
given and never can it be taken back
a magic that's manipulative and cold
when kept to yourself it diminished its purpose
sucks away the magic it possesses
let go and it passes on
either way it is temporary
here and there
then and now
simply loosen the hold
before time more truth will come

04/14/14

Apart from my mind, my body exists. My heart beats. My lungs take in breath and my eyes blink. Apart from my mind, my body is a machine. My mind is my shelter for my questions and doubts. It has the power to distort and create illusions of reality. My mind has a gift of asking me to attain the unmeasurable, the intangible. It can't be calculated. I never win, but my mind is always present, pressing for results with each passing moment. My mind spews lies to my naked eyes. To my own heart, it becomes the whole of existence; distracting the then, disregarding the now. But my body, yes...my body knows the now. My body exists only here, not there. My body knows how to be, but my mind can't. Then, not now, there, not here. If only my mind and body could connect. Then, perhaps a bridge could mend the gap between the two. Together, I may receive some peace and harmony.

05/09/14

devastatingly calm

there's a hush among the dwellers
the hum of silence radiating off their hunched backs
one fidget
one cough
one tear
the hum still remains—devastatingly calm and ever present
as if all contentment and light has been stripped away
there's a calmness—unsettling and beyond the capacity of
words
it's a presence—heavy and suffocating
the dwellers shiver and huddle closer together
a slight rustling of fabric
the shuffling of feet
then the hum—the foreboding silent hum continues
ringing in my ears—in their ears—in its ears
an impending presence beckoning the dwellers toward
disaster
shiver
rustle
they huddle closer together
hum—I feel the silence vibrating in my mind
hum—there are never any answers
hum—the silence is smoke
i turn my back
i walk away
i don't feel
i don't know
i leave them behind
i can't be calm anymore
not now
not ever

05/11/14

Do I even have a purpose?

* * *

06/02/14

My weapon of choice: my mind.

* * *

06/10/14

The things people say only possess as much power as I give them.

* * *

06/15/14

I have been given everything I need to succeed, but I do everything I can to fall on my face. I know it won't work, but I go back every time. My drug. I have chosen emptiness as my one and only drug.

* * *

07/01/14

I admit it; I need someone to fight for me, because the chains wrapped around my neck are so tight I can no longer breathe.

07/14/14

nothing

reality is a loose term
i whisper
i watch my lips move
no sound escapes
the glass shatters
i bleed
real
the blood is real
i lick my finger
with the red liquid I paste my nothingness back together

* * *

07/30/14

i appear

i appear to be moving up
in fact I may be
rising strengthening and growing
i may be rebuilding and slowly changing into a finer version
but version of what
myself
i am not certain
i may be growing stronger evolving succeeding
i may be
so might you

08/18/14

He said the right mind for a man of faith was a mind of faith, and all else was the call of dry realities. And minds so full of questions? How else would faith call to you? Searching within a hopeless soul, it is swallowed by the nothingness— like a lifeless desert starved of rains suddenly flooded by the heavens. Strong, powerful faiths must never be bent by reality's circumstance.

There were few times plagued by a relentless mind that he did not envy those who believed in nothing. So, he took to a doubting mind. Yet, old questions still encroached upon his starving soul.

08/24/14

It is evil. It pulls this young girl toward the bathroom. It has strong arms that reach deep into the girl's pretty face, down her scratched and bleeding throat, forcing her to heave over the porcelain cold seat.

It is evil. It punishes the young girl again and again to purge out her insides until she is hollow, sweaty, and flushed. The young girl collapses to the floor. This is the tenth night that she has slept—sore and beat—curled up around the toilet.

It is evil. It sees the young girl's deteriorating body as a victory. Seeing her presence unravel from the inside out as its only goal. It laughs and dances around the young girl with vomit dried on her chin as it plans how to punish her again tomorrow.

It is evil. Day and night, awake and asleep it consumes, owns, and controls the young girl. It maliciously has taken away all the light from her soul—her smile, her laughter, her passions, her personality. It has left her void. Not a person, just a walking shell. The young girl knows this, yet she cannot seem to escape it…

…Because the evil thing is an eating disorder, and it lives inside her mind.

09/12/14

As today comes to a close, and though I feel incredibly anxious, fat, and sad, I also have a strange feeling of peace. Tomorrow I will get up and try again. Living is trying; anything else is accepting total defeat, and I don't like to lose.

09/27/14

My beauty is perfect.
My beauty is perfect.
My beauty is perfect.
My beauty is perfect.
My beauty is perfect.

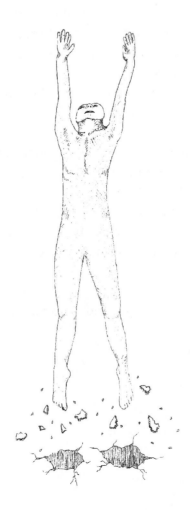

10/01/14

But what does safety bring? Like quicksand, I was stuck: cemented, never growing, never moving—only sinking. Shy, lonely, broken, numb, and starving, I became a slave to my mind. Rules dictated all my actions and shame kept me hidden. Years passed and I only sank lower. Things became darker and my rules grew stricter. My body shrunk smaller, taking with it any memories, emotions, any excitement, any future. I became a number and numbers became me. No identity—just a game, a goal to be beat. The goal became my only companion. All alone; numb; deteriorating. Is this what safety has to offer?

But shy doesn't have to mean forgotten, and lonely is only a state of mind. Anything broken can be mended, numbness screams to be felt, and starvation is not sustainable. Therefore, I am left with risk, change, and faith. I have come to the edge of all I know: the point at which I can either sink until all of me is swallowed or take a leap, trusting that I will learn to fly.

One, two, three…the ground is no more…

10/03/14

If I were to have an endless amount of confidence, I would talk a little louder, stand a little taller, push a little harder, be a little better. With an abundance of confidence, I would no longer hurt my body. There would be no more wishes of starving, or cutting, or harming. No more obsessing, measuring, devaluing. My body would become united with my mind and my mind with my body. With confidence, my eating disorder would cease to be. My mood would improve. My mind would heal. With confidence, I would love and become love. Hatred of my own self wouldn't exist, and wellness would become a possibility. I would have a future, goals, excitement, and freedom. My being would no longer be trapped and life would have purpose again. Because with confidence, I would find the strength to love all the parts of myself, the good and the bad.

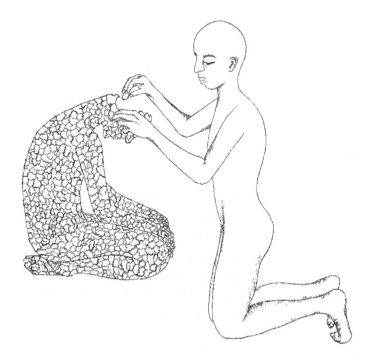

10/04/14

The Girl with China Skin

There was a girl. This girl had a fragility about her, a delicateness to her spirit. She saw the world through a window, staying a safe distance from those who had cracked her fragile china skin. Critical comments over the years had all chipped away at her esteem, nagged at her mind, and left her with a core belief that surely she must hide herself; for no one wishes to be around someone as fragile as her.

The wall was built, gradually; each season brought new bricks and cement. As the years passed, this wall soon became large enough to conceal the girl from the world. Only a window—small and locked—gave the girl a glimpse of what was happening on the other side of the world.

Here, seemingly safe, the girl remained, watching, but never participating, removed, excluded, alone, and with no chance of any more cracks on that china skin of hers. Hidden behind the wall, the girl quickly grew to become her own worst enemy. With no one around, the hurt and pain of the past began to turn inward. Bubbling with emotions, now the cracks were growing larger and larger and larger. Until the day came that her china skin crumbled, shattered to the ground behind the wall she'd built. She laid there alone, no more than a pile of china glass. Shut off from everyone because of the fear of being within. She became her destroyer. The wall that was supposed to bring safety was now catering to her demise.

Time passed, and slowly the wall began to deteriorate. Brick by brick fell in the passing seasons. Until, it became short enough to reveal the very top of the pile of china skin. Now, the girl—for the first time in years—was exposed to those who hurt her in the past. And as those came, they saw the pile of broken china she'd become. Immediately they began to weep, for none of them had any idea that their actions, words, or lack thereof, had proven so detrimental. The girl they had once known had fallen apart right underneath their noses, and not one had been aware. Why hadn't she called out for help, they wondered? But seeing as she was no more, they were left with no explanation. Growing worn by the sad scene before them, they continued on.

More time passed, and the wall eventually fell, ceasing to be. Only the pile of china skin, exposed and alone remained. Until along came a girl, tall, strong, and with a warmth about her. Kneeling by the pile, she reached out a hand. Then, with care and patience, began mending the shattered pieces. It took time, but eventually the girl completed her task. The girl smiled with satisfaction as she moved on from what she had rebuilt. There she was—whole, new, and with shining china skin.

The girl with china skin opened her eyes and looked into the distance

"Hey! Hey! Wait up!" The girl with the china skin called.

The figure in the distance paused and looked back.

The girl gasped because the figure was a mirror whose own face she was staring back at.

10/18/14

Dammit, it's just food!

* * *

10/23/14

As I come to the end of my last night as a teenager, I can't help but reflect on where I am—a residential treatment facility. Never did I think I would spend a birthday locked up because I simply can't eat.

* * *

10/29/14

Don't drink the poison and wait for the other person to die.

* * *

11/03/14

Here I sit. On a bed. In a room with a fan and wooden floors. The door—it creaks. The window-it howls. The bed—it's hard and the lights are dim. My chest rises and falls, rises and falls. This is my life—plain, simple, perpetual. Yes, this is it…the wind, the room, and me.

Me? What an odd concept to grasp. Me with hands and feet and eyes. Me whose lungs breathe again. Me whose heart is still beating, whose blood is still moving, whose mind is still racing.

Here I sit. Very much alive. The fan spins with more direction than me. The wind howls with more purpose than me. The door creaks with more certainty than me.

But me? I am here. I am alive. I am here and I am alive.

I made it through what I assumed to be the worst.

11/04/14

A letter to my five-year-old self:

Dear Child,

Look in the mirror, sweet girl. Put your hands on your soft cheeks. Trace the line your freckles make. Smile, dear child, and see your perfectly imperfect teeth. Those legs, so long and strong. I have seen them run, beating all of the boys in your class. Those graceful arms. Your dancing feet. Unique red hair as if kissed by autumn leaves. Do you see it, little girl? Do you see the strength staring back at you? Those fingers, nimble and precise, with the ability to create amazing things. That stomach, so full of laughter. Those blue eyes. Touch the mirror, child. Come hand in hand. Softly embrace the face staring back at you.

I see innocence not yet tainted by the world. That mind, those experiences, still unblemished. Be open, my child, look now at your hands. Do you know the damage you are capable of? Please, let me hold them, the soft skin warm on mine. Do you know the pain of starvation?

Don't cry, sweet child. Don't let those tears run down your freckled cheeks. Don't let them take away your beauty. Your speckled cheeks and autumn hair. Your chubby legs and dancing arms. Let me dry those tears. Hold your chin up high. You are strong and free. Hear me. Be gentle with the child in the mirror. Touch your hands with grace and dry your tears when sad. Don't follow my ways. You are perfect, child. So dance, and run, and laugh, and sing. Keep being five before a time of insecurity and fear. Dance, little ballerina. Dance for the world so they, too, may see the precious reflection I was once so blessed to know.

11/6/14

in the world there are clouds that move with the wind
i am a cloud
i am a clear sky
i am
i am
I am…

11/8/14

If there was a time when I didn't think I was fat, I don't remember it.

11/14/14

Somewhere over the years, this disease became a fire that I was learning to dance with. It was never fun. It was trapping, engulfing. The fire soon outsmarted my intelligence, growing and burning away at any self I had left.

It is here in the trap of self-loathing I still wallow. Maybe because I don't know anything else, or maybe because my strength is all gone. But hating has become me, and me it. And so it continues, a perpetual cycle, and with every spin, the flame grows larger, and the dance I once knew becomes a race that never ends. I run—round and round and round. I know this trap must collapse one day. I just have to keep running to stay away from its flames.

11/22/14

"How are you feeling?" my therapist asked.

"Joyful, anxious, hurt, grateful, angry, numb, disconnected, hopeful, nauseous, and loved," I said.

"That's a lot for one person," she said.

"I am a lot of person," I told her.

11/28/14

My strive for an extraordinary existence has, up to this point, been through achieving the lowest number on the scale. Because somewhere among my delusions, being the smallest in the room translated to extraordinary. Am I really nothing but a number? Is a number extraordinary enough to fulfill that desire inside me?

I stare at the blinking scale and feel nothing at all.

12/2/14

I am deserving of recovery.

Say it over and over again until it becomes your truth.

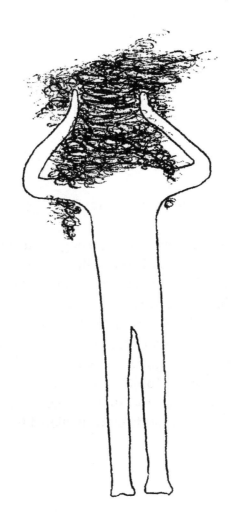

2015: *take away pieces of my eating disorder and PTSD strangles me in its lies, my mom gets sick with metastasized cancer, and my 16-year-old cousin is killed the next week in a tragic car accident, suddenly the world is stronger than my mind*

01/10/15

What does it mean to be in recovery?

Not a place of security, but of change and movement, a process which I take back years stolen. Recovery is now. Recovery is the fight, the fact of deflating the part that is broken and lifting my wellness. Recovery is battling each day, and resting in victory at night. Recovery is falling, crashing, crawling, stumbling, and continuing on. It is a series of acknowledging victories with praise and applause and noticing defeats. To stand for a belief that to keep moving, whether crawling or running, ensures that freedom will meet you on the flipside of the battlefield.

01/12/15

Internally, externally, all of my being, I want to rip at it, cut it, destroy it. I want to shave down my thighs. I want to punch my cheeks until they deflate. I want to disappear when I look in the mirror. Literally, not just in skin and bones. I want to delete my appearance from existence. A black hole; a blank space where it once was. Fill it with nothing, absolutely nothing. I wish, not me, but my body was nothing. Too much pain to look at, too much anxiety to experience. Rip at the flesh, cut it, fix it. Make it feel better! Make my body not hurt so much! Give it scars! Make it bleed! Make it hurt in a way that will heal. Bleed, patch, scab, scar—it's a process, a way for pain to dissipate.

* * *

01/15/15

My skin itches. It calls to me. I break the glass with two pounding fists.

[My demonic hand takes the sharp object.]

A maniac, broken in pieces. I see, blood, warm, tempting. It drips down my skin. My skin itches no more.

02/02/15

I am falling. Falling deeper and more rapidly than my breath can combat. I begin to choke. I need air. Around me is nothing, only darkness. Memories fly past me as I fall.

* * *

02/12/15

These hands—my skin, my arms, legs and stomach, my mind, my eyes, and ears—they are not mine. The monster with its rancid breath and burly arms—it owns me. Over the years, this monster has stolen my health, wellness, and hope. It has stripped me of my identity, and placed it mockingly before me in a wrecked heap of nothingness. Who am I then, if I am not my own? Perhaps I am an opportunity, a heap of rubble to be rebuilt. There are promises to make beauty from the ashes. So do my ashes signify nearness to rebirth? A chance to grow in strength, to become powerful enough to defeat the monster before me and dissipate the nothingness of the ashes that once stood in the way? It all seems a little far-fetched if you were to ask me.

02/16/15

Once written, thoughts become external. Words will never die.

* * *

02/20/15

I am obsessed by an idea. The idea has manifested itself inside my heart, and there it has taken root, spreading through my lungs, stomach, and throat. It has grown so large that it has overtook all my organs and infested every thought and breath I have. The idea is a part of me, a beat from my heart, a freckle on my skin. It is in my inhale, not my exhale. It's in my flexing muscles, in each blink of my eyes. It is in the aroma I smell and the sweetness I taste. The idea contains my essence. It has borrowed my body.

Now, the exact nature of such a possession is complex, offering many layers, which must be extracted in order for comprehension to ensue. Layer upon layer rooted in that ever beating heart, each offering more freedom, less control, and ultimate surrender. One speaks to my eyes, another to my lungs, but the manifestation of all the layers of the entire obsessive idea speaks to my mind, the powerhouse of the machine in which I live. It says, "I have chosen you, child. You are mine." It whispers and every hair on my arms and neck prickles with goosebumps.

The voice that whispers encapsulates all the idea is.

I feel it. Recovery is coming.

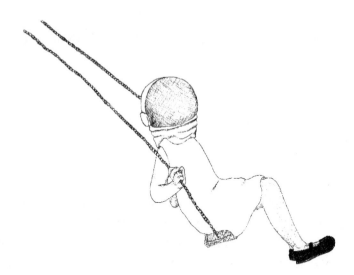

03/08/15

When I was a child, I dreamed of being an astronaut.

* * *

03/17/15

Ever since I was a child, I was a dreamer. Stars, moons, galaxies, fairies, angels, princesses, flying, rainbows, wishes—all mystical and abstract, dominating my imaginative mind. I walk down the street, and I am blinded by the brightness of the sun, deafened by the loudness of the streets, and nauseated by the smells of passing restaurants. I have a gift of heightened sensitivity. The light and dark are debilitating and intense. I feel with the capability of ten minds. I have been shown it is a gift, but a dangerous one.

In middle school, I took a personality test. It told me I was ambitious, goal-oriented, and hard-working. It said these were positive elements, which could work together and ensure my success, but there was a catch. Since I was so driven, the test said that I would always feel like I was falling short of what I envisioned. My expectations were unrealistic, and therefore unattainable. The test spoke a truth, one I knew but had never been able to put into words. One which left me toward tendencies of darker, destructive behaviors. How could I not? To feel with such magnitude is to the world "madness," or rather, "mental illness." We live in a world where you must be okay. But, for me, there is no on/off switch. I am a sponge, constantly absorbing the pain, beauty, and uniqueness of the world.

Am I ill? Am I ambitious? Am I a dreamer? Unapproachable, strange, dangerous?

I am all of these things. My dark inclinations leave me able to access more translucent possibilities. My world is suddenly far more vast than it is to the "sane." I am "mad," as the professionals say, unrealistic to the personality test, and a dreamer to the world. I am to myself, my own, born with a mind with unique capabilities, with depth, with relentless capacity to experience the world around me.

This strangeness about me left my parents a difficult job. I was a loner with her head in the clouds, unresponsive to the norm, and inarticulate in class. I did not believe I belonged in the world, their world, this world. I did not belong. I did not belong. This belief was etched into the concrete core of my being. So that when the concrete dried, the thoughts were permanently ingrained on my pulsing soul. I grew with the world's projections, entangling how I perceived myself. The gift I had was suddenly something that needed to be broken down and swept out. It was wrong. It was destructive. It needed to go. I needed to go.

So I was sent away, my creativity diagnosed as mental illness. Medicated to take away that deep emotional brilliance. I was taught to cope, to be like everyone else, and thrown back into a world I never fit into in the first place.

04/22/15

Over and over again, the necessity of breaking my black and white thinking is reiterated. Therapists, dietitians, psychiatrists, peers—all insist I must learn to live in the gray area of life. I must come to accept that most days are going to rest right there—in the middle, in the mundane, routine, areas of life. I hear this and understand their reasoning, but I can't seem to accept it. If I get rid of the black and white thinking, then why is my eating disorder labeled as black and my true self labeled as white? If I live in the gray, then aren't my eating disorder and I one? So then, can I have both my eating disorder and myself?

05/02/15

Too much, I am far too much. Physically, emotionally, relationally. $X + Y =$ an overwhelming sum. I am in desperate need of subtraction, shrinkage, and disappearance. Written on my bones is this belief, this truth that I must be less to make up for being too much. I am fused with this idea, one with this idea, but what do I do when I exist? When I am here? A being no more or less than those around. I must be. I have no alternative choice. I cannot will my body, mind, soul, and connections with others to disappear. I can't deny that I have a presence in life.

05/15/15

"The soul always knows what to do to heal itself. The challenge is to silence the mind."

-a wise person I don't remember

05/16/15

When my eyes open, I will them to close again to withdraw, to enter back into sleep. Away from the world, the people, the demands, and confusion. Back into my subconscious mind, asleep, vulnerable to my own thoughts—uncharted and uncontrolled thoughts. But, even my sleep is unsafe. When my eyes open, I will them to close again, but opened, closed, what difference does it make? Asleep and awake, in both states, I don't feel okay. My mood is low. I feel alone. I feel hopeless.

07/13/15

minnows

being here
now
on a chair
hearing a harsh woman's voice
many bored faces surrounding
the tick of the clock marking the unraveling of my presence
each moment
piece by piece
falling off my skin
falling like droplets of sweat
landing and then dissipating into a salty sea of pain
into a puddle beneath my feet
a gray-brown color
murky and bubbling
having erupted from the cuts in my fragile skin
there it is beneath my denim worn-out Docs
produced from my scorched soul by years' supply of deeply
rooted worthlessness

i stomp my foot
hard and aggressively
my brown water splashes back onto my wounded skin
the salt stings as it swims upward into my bleeding crevices
the sweat the water's pain is a minnow moving through my
small and narrow veins
an animal living in me borrowing my soul

i stomp again and again
minnows swimming
cuts stinging
painful animals growing within me

i unraveling
sweat dripping
cuts opening
water
brown and repulsive
collecting at my feet

being there
now
on the street
a siren in the distance
cars passing by
the click of the passersby's feet marking the unraveling of
my presence
each moment
piece by piece
falling off my skin
i allow a sea of brown liquid to fill the space around my
worn-out Docs
i allow my cuts to run dry
and the sweat to slow
when passed my being is scorched and depleted
raw and so very drained
yet forward I must trudge through the brown sea of pain
the pain fallen from my seemingly dead dry soul
forward though the sea is choppy and my soul is tired

time has gone and been spent
the tick of the clock no longer marks the crumbling of my
presence
for in time I have grown fins and the sun has turned the
brown waters crystal
my fragile skin has closed the crevices it once left open
my being is sealed and healed beneath its protective coat

i swim as the minnows of pain once moved through my
veins

except now
i
capable and strong
now am the one to disrupt the waters of my pain

07/14/15

"I no longer considered my body my own. It had ceased to belong to me. My hands, moving, felt separate, floating of their own accord, and when I stood it was like operating a marionette, unfolding myself, rising jerkily on strings."

(*The Goldfinch*)

07/23/15

I have been where I am at before. The terrifying part of recovery, where my weight is no longer in my control, and I walk into completely uncharted territory. Every time I have bailed. Run back to my eating disorder. I know where that lands me. So, I stand still. Don't move and pray the circumstances will resolve on their own.

07/29/15

I may be the first to be rained on, but I'll be the last to drown.

08/07/15

I have been asking myself a lot lately why I no longer feel like I am just a shell of a person? Why it is that I don't cry myself to sleep anymore? Or why don't I feel it's necessary to remain silenced by the thoughts and feelings inside of me?

I do, however, still have moments where I am hopeless and dark and feel empty of any goodness, but they aren't my forever, my identity, or my everything. And I have come to the conclusion that hopelessness isn't as romantic as it once was. Hopelessness is easy. It is what I know. It is an empty routine that thrives among seclusion.

I have come to a space where I do not want what is easy. I do not want the rest of my existence to be marked by a series of defeats and destructive behaviors. I do not want to walk down the street praying that this week will be my last. The heavy fog that had come to envelop me over the course of my life has begun to lift. Each time that I have chosen to open my mouth to speak, the fog was penetrated a little more. Those years of being silenced which dictated my existence, my suffering, my darkness, don't have as much power over me. Choices are presented before me, where before, choices were obsolete. My world is a sea of opportunities waiting to be grasped.

I speak and with each sound leaving me, I feel that much fuller, that much more of a person. To hear my voice, have my name called, to hold conversations with someone are all such strange occurrences to me. They let me know I exist when I otherwise doubt so. Stories of my past, things done and not done, are all slowly flowing from my lips. I am sharing them. I am leaving them in places outside of me and that makes me feel...softer. I am no longer a metal sheet unable to bend certain ways without cutting myself.

I have only begun to share bits of my stories. I didn't plan to. In fact, I vowed to myself that I would never speak of these things. I would bury them, get myself healthy, and move on to a better future. But I am talking about them because my therapist doesn't meet me with judgement. I don't shock her. I don't leave fearing what she thinks of me. When I am in the chair in her office, curled up or hiding my face, talking about things that are uncomfortable, I know she gets it.

I think this is why I am starting to feel less of a shell of a person, less like a metal sheet. I have spaces for the things inside my head. Years of being silenced never got me anywhere, and silence only leads me to isolation. It is in isolation that my hopelessness lives, and as I mentioned already, hopelessness is too easy of an option for me.

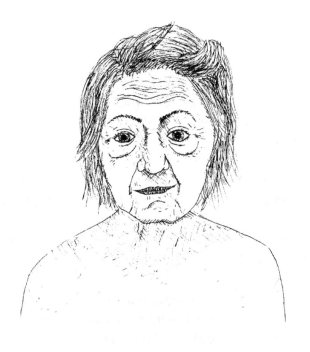

08/10/15

To the old woman with saggy boobs and long hippy hair:

I see a reflection of myself in you. Entangled, we are, in each other's presence. The sway in which you walk, the hunch in your shoulders, the way your unsupported breasts move beneath your purple T-shirt. Your high-waisted, silk pants, and untrimmed hair. You are not like others I may pass. Something fleeting, yet significant, caught my attention. And for that reason, I am connected to you.

We don't know each other. We may never know each other. But we will be entangled in one another, for no reason other than the mere idea that you reflect who I am working to be.

08/15/15

I find comfort in the small spaces. The ones where I can't move and am forced to crunch into a ball. The ones where there are walls on every side of me. The ones where no one can see me, where no one will likely find me. The ones where I can be alone.

I find these are difficult to come by here. There are too many people running around me, too many things happening, too much stimulation. A conversation I can't hold. A sound I can't hear. A scene I can't process. My mind is somewhere else. My mind is not twenty. My mind does not know time.

I try to escape for a moment, to a corner in the room—not my room, but our room. It is here, curled tight into a ball that I hide. In my lap, I hold a stuffed bear. I clutch my fists and eyes. My body is scared. My body feels. My body is hurting. My body brings me pain.

I am in two places. Scared and not. An adult, safe with choice. A child, scared and compliant.

I don't move. I won't move. I can't move.

The smaller I feel, the less of a person I am, the less of a presence the sensations can maintain, the less weight the memories may hold. Smaller and tighter and tenser. I remind myself of where I am in case I leave, in case I go back to that kitchen, that bathroom, that yelling face…the time, the next time, the three times…

Please, no one find me. No one see me. No one come to know what is happening inside me.

08/23/15

The sky was a giant mess of gray cotton balls spitting down at me. The wind blew with a chilling sting, meant to shock my deadened presence. The lake was sad. Each time the old fishing boat rocked—*back and forth, back and forth*—I could hear the waters whimpering, a baby cry that deep in my belly I knew was my own. Each splash sank into my pores and became a part of me, the whimpers softening as they found a warm and silent home.

I was not disappointed in the weather, for to be out in the sun and warmth would have felt forced. In the overcast, I felt connected with the surrounding waters. The whimpers called to me. The other divers didn't seem to notice, but I heard them. I heard their sadness and for that reason I believe the waters were grateful to have me. We were different manifestations of the same state of being.

With my fins on, my weight belt in place, and my regulator in my mouth, I stepped off the back of the boat and into Lake Michigan. The sad waters rapidly etched their way through the layer of space between my skin and wetsuit. A chill radiated through my body, and my breath became short and harsh. In a large gasp, a pool of water entered my mouth. My body rejected it, coughing and panting even more. My warm breath fogged up my mask and my regulator was lost somewhere in the space beside me. I could not see, my body was shaking, and my lungs were screaming for warm air.

But then, something shifted. As soon as I began my descent, not even three feet below the surface, the environment changed. No longer were there choppy waves and spitting rains. No longer was their wind. No longer was there anything. And it was here that I paused, long enough for the whimpering call that I previously felt so connected with to ring through my ears. There was that warm sound, that true sound, able to create a sensation deep in my belly, which could radiate back up calmness and understanding. Suddenly, the waters didn't seem so cold, because inside I was warm and my lungs were able to receive the cool air with gratitude. My regulator somehow found its way back to my mouth, and my body no longer panting; I was able to clear my mask. The space around the divers and I was endless. It was this overwhelming vastness that I found so welcoming. Below was nothing but a drop into deep green waters. I was a speck in the midst of everything. Black. Bobbing. Bubbles rising to the surface. A foreigner to the space around, yet ever connected in a transcendent way.

I could have stayed there, unmoving, unchanging, simply relishing in this feeling. I was nothing, but this made me significant. For, under the surface, there were no words. You are void of the constraints of air and land and the obligations they bring. Under the surface, the ultimate goal is to be aware of where you are at the given moment. A diver can find connection in vastness, and I don't have to be a different manifestation from the waters which housed me. For here, the waters and I are the same. I am not overlooking them from a rocking fishing boat. I am in them, with them. I am them. The waters sink into my exposed skin and stay as a part of me, warming the space deep in my belly. I am able to breathe in their sadness, become the sadness while being at peace within myself. Under the surface, sadness is not negative. It is a state of being. It is how the water feels on my skin. It does not make me feel heavy or tearful, but content in resting where I am at.

08/28/15

I am having those thoughts again. The thoughts that I am no good, that I am nothing, that everyone would be better off without me. I can't move. Paralyzed by sadness. Loneliness lies heavily on my shoulders. I am nothing. Crushed under the weight of isolation.

I have been locked in a box. The box is small and I am large. Discomfort becomes my normal. Silence is my sole name. There is no door. The box was built around me when I was small. Time spent. I have grown and no longer fit. I am heavy inside the box, pushing against the weight of the metal walls. *Someone please let me out.* I don't have a voice. No sound leaves my lips. No sound leaves the walls.

I am lying in my bed, wrapped tightly in the covers. The stuffed animals surrounding my body protect me. I don't trust myself to move. I don't. I cry—a heaving, deep belly cry that has been building up for so long. Much has come and gone, been done and not done. Tears organically stream, telling the world of all my wrongs.

I am alone. Darkness outside. Darkness inside. Inside me. *Alone. Alone. Alone.* The word haunts me. Mocks me. My box seems ever smaller. My heaving lessens. The apartment's eerie silence fills the space.

I am scared. Scared of myself—my thoughts, my capabilities, my past. I can't fall asleep. I can't get up. I don't move. Fear and shame keep me hidden deep inside my covers. I will myself to disappear, never to return to the world. The night is long. Time to deem myself invisible. The world will sleep. I will not. Fear steals all comfort from me.

09/03/15

I have two selves.

The outward self—the one that wears weird clothes. The one that likes chokers, who makes jokes when uncomfortable, who thrives in the ability to act according to the space she's in.

The hollow self—the shell that my personhood has been taken from. The hollow self has endured a lot, survived a lot, but at a great cost, for nothing remains inside the shell. Hollowness. Emptiness. This self is fragile and broken.

Now, I have been working on both selves. The outward self has grown in size and spirits. Success, I would say. The hollow self has begun to move, and in the movement, has gained a little strength. And in that little strength came a small, small voice. A whisper. A whisper that gave hint to those who have sucked out the person that once occupied this shell.

But the environment is shifting. The outward self remains true. Go to school. Get dressed. Smile. Be a part of the world around. The hollow self-panics. She stops moving—freezes mid stride and retreats into her shell. The voice is swallowed, the whispers only of the passing wind. Silence. Hide. One self is now mobile, and the other…stagnant.

09/15/15

They all work against me, dictating my actions, my thoughts, my beliefs. Pulling in every which way, I am a puppet dancing around and around, up and down, twirling, and then falling. There is a string connected to every point on my body each directed by a different puppeteer. I am unable to disobey. I am not my own. I am theirs. The impulses created by their strings govern me, make me, mold me. Until, resistance builds in the form of shutting down.

I curl up on the floor. A ball, small and child-like, with her eyes closed. I am left alone and tired. Played and beat. I cut the strings and tie them around my body, creating my own net, my own cage. My own. Even without the puppeteers, I still choose for the impulses to become me. I allow them to debilitate me. I can't move when tied up. Weak. Under a web of string. Alone and motionless I remain trapped in the net of my own arms. Here, I am at peace.

09/17/15

"Never be bullied into silence. Never allow yourself to be made a victim. Accept no one's definition of your life, but define yourself."

— Harvey Fierstein

* * *

09/18/15

Now I can begin. All my mistakes up to now are teaching me the picture I must paint.

09/18/15

Snakes crawl up the goddess's legs and onto her torso. They wrap themselves tightly around her shoulders, entangling her with their long bodies. Tighter they wind themselves until all the air is squeezed from the goddess's lungs, and nothing stronger than a faint whimper can leave her lips. Steam exudes from her ears as she grows hot in the desert air. No sweat drips from her brow. She has no moisture to spare.

The snakes are the arms of her destroyer. He found her despite running away to the desert - this barren ground with no water or life. She ran to escape his relentless chase, but no time or space can shield the goddess from him—the destroyer is from a realm that exceeds understanding. A liminal realm where constraints of life do not own him. In fact, the destroyer's life takes life, and the goddess's youthful spirit proved a delicious ownership for the destroyer's shadow.

The snakes coiled ever tighter and the goddess collapsed. Beat. Defeated. It was here when the goddess was no longer able to fight, she realized the snakes were her own arms. In surrendering, she was able to feel the sublimity of release.

09/24/15

hypervigilance

                                                                    unknown

                                                        night time

                            closed
                box
        trapped

                            nowhere
                                no one
                                        nothing
                        empty
                    stomach
            toilet
                porcelain

                                        cold

sad

                                                                    exhaust
                                                                    ed

                                                    V
                                            O
                                    M
                        I
                T

09/26/15

when you cry from deep in your belly
and your sobs turn into heaving
and your body is clenched with no hope of tasting a breath

when you can bathe in the tears pouring from your eyes
and the saltwater burns as it leaks onto your chapped lips
and it tastes like a heavy sad ocean on your dry dry tongue

when you lie on your bathroom floor with the lights off
and you sob until you physically can't anymore
and you're nothing more than flesh flickering in your candle's light

when your thoughts swim to the dialogue of *too much*
and that your body is too much
        and you are too much
                and life is too much
                        and hoping is too much
                                and thinking is too much

when you have that night that you don't think you can survive
and you fall asleep
and when you wake up you find a way to begin again

09/28/15

I feel uncomfortable and anxious and conflicted and confused and disgusted and incompetent and unwanted and scared. I feel like a radioactive ball of nuclear materials that is buzzing with an eccentric energy, and is proving to be a hazard to people around. I feel like I am a psychic's crystal ball, where I am indefinitely shifting colors so no predictions can be made. I feel like a thunderstorm in the summer—loud and destructive, but terrifyingly beautiful. I feel like a puppy with fleas that desperately wants to be snuggled with, but no one can go near because it is infectious.

This has been my problem all day. I am feeling too many things. I cannot focus on one task for more than thirty seconds. In fact, I am writing this while also listening to music, drinking hot chocolate, texting, making a To Do list, checking my email, and reading an article for school. The reason for these incessant, racing thoughts and attempts at multitasking is that I am at a high risk for self-destruction. Why? Because I am caught up in the past. I am caught up in past hurts and past failures and past mistakes that I have made—all things that make me feel deserving of punishment.

But if there is one thing I have learned over the past few years, it is that you can think—and maybe even believe one thing—and act opposite to those thoughts. So for now, despite my crazy busload of emotions and self-deprecating thoughts, I will just finish writing.

10/06/15

An excerpt from Frederick Buechner's novel, *Brendan:*

Pushing down hard with his fists on the table top he heaved himself up to where he was standing. For the first time we saw he had one leg. It was gone from the knee joint down. He was hopping sideways to reach for his stick in the corner when he lost his balance. He would have fallen in a heap if Brendan hadn't leapt forward and caught him.

"I'm as crippled as the dark world," Gildas said.

"If it comes to that, which one of us isn't, my dear?" Brendan said.

Gildas with but one leg. Brendan sure he'd misspent his whole life entirely. Me that had left my wife to follow him and buried our only boy. The truth of what Brendan said stopped all our mouths. We was cripples all of us. For a moment or two there was no sound but the bees.

"To lend each other a hand when we're falling," Brendan said. "Perhaps that's the only work that matters in the end."

10/07/15

minefield

close your eyes and let me take you to the world I know
dead grass of a stark barren field
black crows an emblem cooing over nothingness
a vortex of cries endlessly reverberating over your shaken
bones
digest the darkness before taking a step
swim in the darkness
hold it as it pierces your searching hands
suffocate in the blood soaked fog
swallow the remains of once was

where you are standing is a minefield
one step could signify the end
walk on glass
breathe in crimson
listen to the orchestration of danger's call
everything becomes nothing
nothingness becomes your shield
to hold it is to never lose
shield in hand a breath tasting of invincibility propels you
forward
unfortunate as the single step activates the darkness to
pierce your every part
a minefield of unpredictability
the one step holds the one thing you still own

your existence

10/07/15

My belly is swelling. Not out of discomfort, not out of grief or fear or sadness, not out of bloating from a meal. My belly is swelling with delight, with an overwhelming sensation of gratitude, with an abundance of connectivity. My insides aren't just filled, but overflowing. They have become a rushing river filling me with rejuvenation. I can only explain it as this: I have surpassed my capacity of joy.

Tears have formed in the corners of my eyes where saltwater has, in the past, refused to accumulate. Little drops of clear liquid to show the immensity of this time in space. This space is liminal; it does not operate under the constraints of reality. This space surpasses any previous reality I have come to know. Here, a moment of visible strength, a moment where *I am* a moment—where I am connected, where I am seen, where I am known.

My belly is swelling because I have felt what it is like to be seen as a person.

10/08/15

Two years ago in November, I walked into treatment for the first time. First time in treatment, first time meeting with a therapist, first time in therapy groups. Since then, I have met eight different therapists and six dietitians. Move to IOP, get a new therapist, move to PHP, get a new therapist, move to residential, new therapist. I have been tossed from team to team every couple of months, never allowing myself to build a connection with them, knowing that in a few months they would leave. But I never challenged this because it is what I am used to. Instability, people coming and going, learning to hold your own unpredictability—these are all things I know. It wasn't until recently that I began to see fault in this aspect of my treatment, because in having therapists and dietitians come and go all the time, my treatment team is mimicking my own disorder.

10/10/15

there is something about the okay
the average
the normal
that reminds me of the water

there is something about the not quite
the almost
the little bit longer
that feels like I am swimming

there is something about the routine
the everyday
the schedule
that mimics the sound of waves

there is something about ordinariness of my life
that leaves me drowning in the water
flailing in the depths
and thrashing in the waves

to thrive in the ordinary only happens
when you fall limp and let the current rule
my struggling body moves against
i'd rather fight than accept the ocean's rule

10/11/15

sometimes i enter a time of haze
i can't see in front or behind
i wave my hand
i fling my arms
they become nothing more than moving masses
engulfed in a fog
the fog blinds or rather impairs
i feel lost
dazed
dreaming
what's to come
my mind is blank
blank
blank from opinion
blank from desire
blank from goal
blank because it cannot be decided
too conflicted too clouded
i am torn
too confused to pick a side
move onward stay or go backward
the choice should be simple
live or die
isn't that the real question
let it go
but i can't
i am too fused with the thoughts
they define my entire existence
dictate my thoughts
they are me
physically
mentally
emotionally

even spiritually
how does one alter their existence
is such a thing even achievable
i don't know
so i stay wallowing in the haze
conflicted and my mind ever more blank

10/13/15

I know — or at least I have been told — that the substance the silkworm discharges while making his cocoon would poison him if he kept it inside. He purges himself of it. To save himself, he empties himself. The cocoon, which he is obliged to form under threat of death, and which he would be unable either to imagine to fashion otherwise, protects the metamorphosis of the caterpillar. The caterpillar can't become a butterfly unless emptied of that silky poison.

10/30/15

My body is tired. My mind is full. My heart is heavy. So heavy. So very heavy. I could collapse under its weight. Collapse and crumble into a pile. A large pile. A pile of obstacles. Obstacles, meaning hardship. And by hardship, I mean pain. The pile of my existence equals hurt. That is too pessimistic, too depressing. Not hurt, perhaps misfortune.

I crumble because I am ice. A sculpture of ice as fragile as glass. Melt me. You can't. My soul has died inside my chest. I am slowly freezing from the inside out. You can't melt me. Even the hottest of flames would do nothing. But shatter me. That is inevitable. It already happened. I have shattered.

> *Shattered.*
> **Shattered.** I am a pile. A pile of glass, of ice, of hollow pieces.

I am really sad. My tears are sharp. I am ice and I cry glass. My tears cut my cheeks. Streams of red fall beneath the shards that pile at my feet. When I cry, I make no sound. Digesting my cries is the only way. The right way. The true way. What is the way? Ways are indefinable. Right. Left. Up. Down. The world is dimensional. My life is dimensional. It used to be one layer. Now, there are many.

11/05/15

hollow

i carry the weight of my
existence on broken arms
the air is a cloud of toxic smoke
that forcibly engulfs
me in a blanket of haze
it plays with my mind until it spins like a top and
becomes a bowling ball thrown at crystal

> *shattered*
>> into a million hollow pieces

scramble to get far far away.
until i am teetering on one foot atop a flagpole
where the cold winds are hard wearing
and i slowly freeze from the inside out
icicles form around my lungs
soon my soul will die inside my chest
and i will become as the crystal

> *shattered*
>> into a million hollow pieces

11/09/15

There is nothing like when you feel nothing, know nothing, experience nothing. And nothing about that previous sentence probably made any sense, but that is precisely the point. Nothing makes sense if you really think about it.

My eating disorder doesn't make sense. I am afraid of calories, and my weight, and the measurement of my thighs. I obsessively think about the number of carbs in my cereal, or the grams of fat on my sandwich. When I go to the gym, I stare at the numbers as if they are going to reach out and grab my throat. Numbers dictate a huge amount of my thoughts. Is it 12:30 a.m. or 12:33? I need to know the exact times. 72 percent on my paper or 74 percent? I need to know the exact grades. Did I leave for class at 8:32 a.m. or 8:33? I have to know. None of it makes any sense and slowly I have begun to peel myself away from my neurotic obsession with numbers.

My mom having cancer doesn't make sense. She is a good person. She is my mom and I need her. I need her to be around. I need her to call me and talk to me and let me know that everything is okay. I need to know that my mom is okay. And right now, I don't know that. I don't even know if the treatment is going to work. I don't know anything, and that is the worst position to be in. Helpless. Waiting. Offering nothing but love.

Love doesn't make sense. It is this strange and beautiful thing that is not confined by the constraints of this world. It exists in its own realm. It transcends all understanding. Love is unexplainable, and therefore the closest thing we have to magic. Love can heal all brokenness. I believe in a Higher

Power that can heal all brokenness. All hurt and pain. They can dry all the tears.

My God doesn't make sense. That is why they are God and I am a human. They are bigger than all things. I will never understand their path. I will never understand anything about them. My God loves me, and I love my mom, and love is magical. It has the power to heal all kinds of sickness. That's how I know we will all be okay. Nothing makes sense. Things are not okay. But we will be okay because we have the universe on our side.

11/15/15

I wish that I could shrink like I used to. I wish that I could choose that path again, but it would be too embarrassing, too humiliating. I have come too far to turn back. Far enough to get fat. They say we aren't going to make you fat, and then one day you wake up and realize that is exactly what happened. Your biggest fear has come true. *What ever happened to self-control? What ever happened to thin? To small? To shrink? To disappear? What ever happened to wanting to be small so that there would be less of your body to deal with?*

My body holds too many memories. Too many things are tied to it. I want a new one. I want out of my own skin. Where is the zipper to the winter coat I am wearing? Oh wait, this extra layer is now permanently attached to my skin. What have I done? What have I become? What is this chaos and life around me, but a series of unfortunate events? My body is repulsive and my life is chaotic. Nothing seems right. Nothing seems okay. I want to be thin. I want to feel bones and not the rolls on my stomach.

I want my mom to just be my mom. Not sick. I just want everything to be okay and it isn't.

11/19/15

Rushing rushing water blue gray yellow sun hope light me you us them family vacation ocean diving sharks fish Bahamas oxygen air nothing gasping paranoia sick death dark cancer chemo surgery catheter urine blood smells sadness tears tired exhaustion beds scratchy sheets hope none me and my mom my mom and me I want to be with my mom Netflix soup vomit *pain pain pain pain* excruciating help prayers release please *help help help* holding guiding washing rubbing praying talking sleeping eating panic fat *gross gross gross* I am so gross food calories exercise *run run run* keep running until you feel nothing void no tears I don't feel anything I want to be with my mom I want to be with my mom I want to be with my mom she just had surgery and I should be with her why did I come back to Chicago nothing here matters that is a lie I care about Chicago I care

about my team and my friends and my school actually I
don't have any friends I never have never will I am a loner
but what does that matter I don't care if I am my mom
doesn't care if she is we are the same in that way we can
relate on so many levels I love my mom I love my mom I
don't want to lose my mom please God don't take her from
me so much love so much confusion so much pain I don't
know what to do with myself there is too much to feel too
much to know too much to not know we don't know
anything nothing is in our control anymore it is up to faith
and God and prayers so I pray all the time when I am
walking when I am peeing when I am eating I pray for my
mom because I need her to get better because I need her in
my life we all do my sister brother especially dad he needs
her so badly he doesn't know what to do right now he is out
of his element he is not a caregiver our caregiver is sick none
of us know what to do we are all fish out of water confused
and scared and unable to breathe God grant us serenity we
all need it.

12/04/15

I will never forgive God for having to write these words:

Andy is dead.

12/12/15

i didn't know i could shed so many tears
until an ocean of saltwater flooded my bathroom

i didn't know that i could hurt so badly
until this pain in my chest left me wailing on the floor

i didn't know that i could keep breathing without him
until his presence in me was violently removed

i didn't know that a person could stare at a wall for so many
hours
until it was midnight and i felt no sense of passing time

i didn't know the hollowness of raw heartbreak
until i witnessed the bleak crater it left in my chest

i didn't know the true act of surrender
until i was forced to fall on my hands and knees

i didn't know a lot of things
until the day i lost him and began falling
                and falling

                        and falling

                                        endlessly
                        falling

i didn't know how to trust that there was a bottom
until i heard his small whisper in my ear *Make It Count*

i don't know when i will find bottom
but i have his last words there to lend me some faith that
there is one

12/16/15

i want to be so self-aware that i can be completely unaware of self

i want to be so transfixed on love and peace and freedom that these spiritual elements become tangible

i want to search so fervently for these elements that i am fully conscious of their presence in me and in those around me

i want to wake up and look in the mirror but find no concern for the outline of the self but see the housing for my soul

i want to get up and skip the mirror because my eyes have finally been silenced

i want my eyes to become blind to the world and opened to another dimension that will offer me a purpose and an overwhelming sense of hope in the midst of turmoil

i want to be able to stand up in front of people and honestly say that i lost someone i love but am finding peace within the circumstances

i want to know this state of acceptance so that i can see Andy's love left behind

i want to be able to see Andy's love because i am so in touch with the spiritual world that his love becomes a blanket and this blanket is red and vibrant and covering the entire body I want it to be real so very real

i want this so that when i take the blanket to my chest it softens the icicles around my heart

i want the ice to melt as his warmth now floods my lungs

i want the blanket—the tangible expression of Andy's legacy—to be where i find what love and peace and freedom feel like

2016: *dissecting my head and purging an endless array of thoughts, while swimming through a shit ton of struggles and trying to manage recovery alongside a drowning mind*

01/19/16

Between the constant battle among my mind and body and the show I put on for all the people around me, I'm always exhausted. Relentlessly, unendingly, perpetually exhausted. Every day, faced with the same battles, the same insecurities, the same self-deprecating thoughts. I start spiraling into a place of darkness, a place where I believe that the damage done over the years is permanent—that I am irreversibly spoiled and terminally broken.

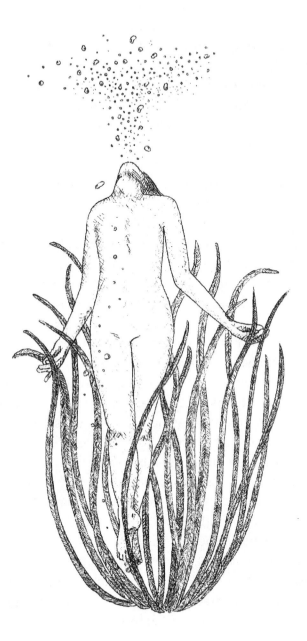

01/20/16

The ocean is the space I escape to when I am in distress. Deep in my mind, I hold onto the feeling of the water rushing over my face as I jump off the boat dock. I hold onto the stillness of my body as I descend down to the ocean floor. No one can talk under the water. No words, no noise—just the steady sound of my own lungs filling and emptying. The bubbles that ascend from my regulator tell me that I am seen in this space, that my mass is known, that I take up space. Unlike on land, where the world is dictated by words and conversations, I am important down under the water. Silence is known under the water.

When my body is suspended in the water, I know I am held. The current will carry me. The water will envelop me. The ocean embraces me simply because I am there, because I jumped into the water, because I am swimming.

The water turns the life around me a tint of blue. The stingrays and sharks, the fish and the coral are brighter than anything you would see on the surface. I see fish with scales of the brightest pink, of the deepest purple. I touch sharks with deep and jagged scars just like the ones I wear on my legs. The world on the ocean floor is special. Only a few get to witness it. I get to witness it because the ocean invited me to lunge beneath its surface. It graciously allows me, a human, to intrude on a world where humans don't exist. Weight doesn't matter under the surface because the saltwater leaves you weightless. Words don't matter because words cannot be spoken. My past isn't with me because no fish or shark or stingray knows the meaning of the word *trauma*. Under the surface I am just a living thing. I am me and I am welcomed to be that.

The therapist running this group told us to describe our compassionate space. Well, if the ocean is not the definition of compassion, then I don't know what is.

01/28/16

I soak my meals in blood as I force them down my throat.

01/29/16

fragments

fragile lips
taste dry cotton
red stained
to be swallowed
penetrated esophagus
burning lungs
drowned in freezing waters
pale frozen skin
soul of solid ice
an abyss of frozen paralysis
infinitely blank space

nothing

crossroads of despair
gyrate a cocoon
wrapped in cellophane
revolving discs
purple deflated domes
an archway to hell
thrust forward
razor blades
lean into cutting
pain is euphoric

my enchanted world.

02/02/16

When I first walked into the room of couches and had an IV of compassion stuck inside my veins, they told me my eyes were broken. Distorted, sick, not right—they are a disillusioned gateway into the physical world. I said they aren't because how could they be? I saw color and shape and depth and beauty all around. It was not what I looked at from afar that was wrong. It was not my friends, or my family, or strangers on the street that I pointed at and screamed, but me—the face reflected back at me in the mirror. The one with the hollow, empty eyes and swollen cheeks. The one who seems to blow up the longer I stare, until she is filling the entire bathroom. A massive form growing and growing, forever growing because she has to in order to contain all of the pent up anger, sadness, grief, and heartbreak. They told me my eyes were broken, so I turned off all the lights to keep myself from catching a glimpse of that hollow child ever again.

The cycle of couches became routine. Kleenex and Ensures, exchanges and process. They told me I was getting stronger, and I could turn the light switch back on. But, when I tried no light filled the space. The electricity had been cut. The fuse was left unfed for too long. It was severed, no longer responsive to my finger's touch. They told me my fingers were broken. I refused to believe them. I used to drive myself to the brink of insanity fighting with the switch. Yelling and screaming, kicking and punching because it should work god damn it! It should work! But time passed, and desires shifted, and I stopped wishing for the switch to turn back on. It was then that I found the real light, the one outside of my window. The ball of fire barely peeking over the horizon. The sun. It has been stuck there for a long time, failing to rise, but resting far enough so that I knew it is there and that there was a promise of light coming soon. They told me this was an awakening. I told them my fingers should work now. They told me they were still broken. To look at the sun and not the switch because my hand was not the answer. Outside of myself. Outside of my room, my switch, my mirror, and my face—that is where I would find the fix. It wasn't my eyes that were broken, but my heart. Only a whole heart could mend it, could share enough to patch mine so that it could remain beating. Outside of myself, because everything inside is short fused and apparently broken.

My heart keeps growing despite the pain. I tell it to stop, but it says it is not me who gets to decide. It is the past hurts, the past memories, the past mistakes, the past highs, the past loves that decide what size is required of the muscle. My heart is so large it was hard to house inside a hollowed body. So I had to grow. I had to eat and grow because I needed a space for that abnormally huge muscle. I didn't want to, but I did because if I didn't, I would die. Not just physically, but mentally, emotionally, and spiritually. I needed to grow because my spirit was very much alive.

They tell me my story will heal me. I tell them that is not the case. They assure me it is part of the journey. I tell them I would rather look the other way. They tell me that I have already turned the lights off. For once, they are right. The only light left was the one on the horizon, the hope and peace—the one that is inextinguishable because it is out of my reach. That light is never ceasing and that terrifies me. That light shines through to my heart. That light is what is feeding the muscle and therefore has become the reason for its eternal growth. My broken fingers can't touch the light and kill it. My broken eyes can't falsely know it because it is far outside of me. Far enough that it is real.

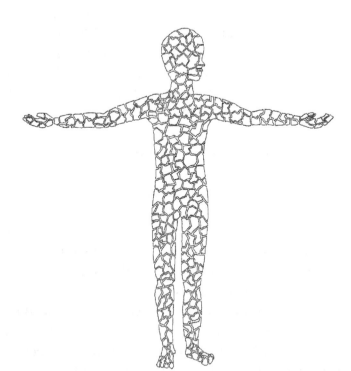

02/08/16

At birth, every person in this world is a flawless slab of glass. Clear, smooth, a frame of translucency and fragility. But as we move through life, nicks, cracks, and sometimes even bullet holes mark up our glass, leaving areas damaged and dangerous. Dangerous, because it is a known fact that glass, when broken, cuts. Now, some people experience more cracks in their slab of glass than others. Some even come to a point in their lives where their entire slab is shattered and not a single crevice resembles the original flawless glass that their existence once was.

People make cheesy statements about how "you have cracks so the light can shine in," and "people who have more cracks are able to shine brighter." Or the quote "she never seemed shattered. To me she was a breathtaking mosaic of battles she had won". I can say that I agree with these cheesy quotes, not because I have seen them personally play out in my life, but because I have to believe in them in order to keep moving. Because the moment I stop and decide that my shattered piece of glass is just broken and will always be broken and there is no way to find beauty in it, I lose all hope in my pursuit of emotional healing.

This doesn't negate the fact that being a shattered slab of glass hurts. Sure, you can paint it in attempt to create a stunning stained glass window out of your brokenness that has ten times more light peeking through it than the person next to you who only has one little crack in her slab. But still it hurts to be a stunning stained glass window, to be cracked, to be a beautiful rendition of what was supposed to constitute the end of your existence. There is something incredibly powerful about rebuilding your slab to reinvent it from the pure, perfect existence it once was into a collection of nicks, cracks, and bullet holes that now are uniquely complex and direct reflections of your experiences. Still, we all know that broken glass cuts. So those of us who feel as though our past experiences have shattered parts, if not all of our existence, it is because we know that each movement hurts.

The waters of our showers are acidic. The mattresses on which we sleep are lined with nails. The backpacks we walk to work with are loaded with five insanely heavy boulders. The days are hard. Arbitrary tasks become burdensome. Breathing becomes exhausting, but no one knows. Because to everyone around, we are a beautiful mosaic of strength.

We are overcomers and survivors caked in resilience. The pain is in the space between the mosaic pieces—the cracks whose edges are marked by sharp shards of blood and tears. Those are the parts that cut at the light streaming in; those are the parts that leave us hurting. But those are the parts that become a beacon of hope to everyone else.

There is a reason why we search for emotional healing, whether from past traumas or mental illnesses such as an eating disorder, or depression, or anxiety, or tragic losses, or chronic illness, or anything in between. There is a reason why it is the very nature of humanity to create, fix, render, and grow—we want to understand the meaning of all this pain. We want to understand why some of us have more cracks than others. We want to make sense of it all. So we take those cracks, and reframe their meaning. They are the spaces where light shines through. They are the spaces that act as the foundations for mosaics and stained glass windows created from our pain. And somehow, the reframing of the brokenness makes it all bearable. It makes the acidic showers, nail-lined mattresses, and boulders on our backs somehow less painful. It makes all of this hurt we have endured worth it, to have someone else look at our glass and think it is beautiful.

02/10/16

Tonight I went on a treasure hunt. I do this sometimes. Wander around the city without direction or time constraints, seeing what little gems I can find while blasting inspirational songs in my Beats.

I am an alumnus to my past treatment center, so I get to go to alumni events. No longer do I schedule into my week therapy groups and supported meals. No longer do I crave the comfort of being told what to eat and when to eat it. No longer do I feel like I am splitting in two, unless I have that space filled with couches and teary faces to validate my week's pain. I am an alumnus and I haven't been able to say that in over two years so it is an empowering identity to take on. To celebrate, I went on a treasure hunt because treasure hunts are special and only happen when the inspiration strikes me.

Staring up at the tall buildings, feeling the February air brush against my cheeks, my music drowning out any city noise, I was in a time warp, a liminal space, alone in a bustling world, one among two hundred million. I was here and not at the same time, because my heart was connected in that moment with my spirit—my spirit being the part of me that notices my purpose is bigger than what I see in the mirror. That my body is simply a vessel for this endless liquid that contains my soul, and my vessel was flooded with the waters of my soul because I was able to open the lid to the bottle gifted by my spirit. I was, for a moment, overwhelmed by the beauty of this life, this world, this body, this mind given to me. For a moment, I was drowned in contentment with all that has and will happen. For a moment, I felt completely at peace.

These moments are fleeting—as they should be. No person could sustain that state of wonder and connection for their entire existence, and if that was their entire existence, then it wouldn't be full of wonder and connection. The experience of the spirit and the soul wouldn't even be beautiful because it would just be. Nothing more. Nothing less. In order to appreciate these mountain top moments, I have to know what valleys, dungeons, raging rivers, and vast canyons feel like. I have to know the good, the bad, and the ugly in order to appreciate everything beyond and in between.

I am an alumnus because I was once a patient awaiting an intake session, I am a treasure hunter because I was once buried in a garbage dump, and I experience the filling of my soul because I know what it is like for my body's vessel to remain an empty shell.

02/12/16

I binged and I purged and I am sorry for the pain it is going to cause tomorrow. I will get up and I will have breakfast. I will do my homework. I will go to my internship. I will be with the artists. I will go to therapy, but I cannot guarantee truthfulness.

Purging, the act of emptying myself, there is no justifying that slip. I just had to. I can't give an explanation. I just had to. There was no other choice. I wouldn't have been able to continue on this week at school or at work or with friends without this slip. I was lying to myself, and this slip felt like the truth. Forcing myself to vomit felt like justice for all that has been done. No one is there to know. No one can offer that escape from this mind of mine.

I am trapped in destructive thoughts and beliefs. All I want is to curl up and never look at anything again because the images of this world only remind me of the world that was taken from me, the world of acceptance and love that I could have had. A world I never came to know. Now I am damaged beyond what even my therapist can see. I am cut deeper and further than words can describe. I don't know if I will ever recover. I don't know if I can ever find a way to be whole.

How does a mosaic come to find peace with the cracks? How do I find peace with the notion that I am always going to hurt, that this pain will always be here? I don't want to feel this way anymore. I don't want these memories anymore. But they are part of my story, they come with me everywhere. Why was I gifted this extra luggage?

I don't know how to be better. I don't know how to find recovery. I don't know how to let go of the past. It haunts me. It haunts me in the day and in the night. Awake and asleep. I can't find any peace. Help me. But there is no one there to help. God is there. I know they are and yet, I shut them out because I don't want them to see me destroy myself again. I shut the door because I don't want my sister or my brother or anyone to see me as I shove a toothbrush down my throat and vomit until there is nothing left, and find pride in the little white pieces of my stomach lining still floating in the toilet. I am killing myself. I know that, and yet I can't find a reason to stop. I am killing myself and I am okay with that, and I know that if I tell anyone they will think I am crazy. They will tell me to get help. They will tell me I am throwing my life away. And I can't explain to them that my life was already thrown away years ago, that I never actually wanted this life. That I am nothing more than a quiet, little girl with no backbone of her own. I don't see the possibilities for myself because possibilities are only a cover up for the emptiness I feel inside.

I will make art. I will help people. I will pray to God. I will go to therapy, but I don't feel healed inside. I don't feel like I am moving. I am fixing, putting tape on top of deep deep wounds. I am not healing. My healing won't come because you can't prune parts of yourself that were never grown. That is like telling someone without an arm to exercise it, and it will feel better. Get in touch with your authentic self—as if I have one. But I don't. I wonder if all those who were sexually abused feel like they don't have a self?

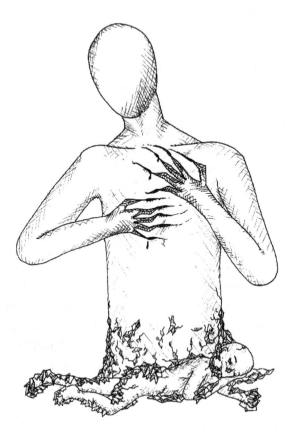

02/15/16

Defining PTSD:

Flashback.

It was cold, bone cold, so cold that all things seemed to shut down and I wasn't sure. Sure about the day, or the time, or whether the cloud of breath illuminated beneath the street lamp was mine. It was silent, a short-lived kind of silence, wherein each brief moment of quiet passed before a cluster of noise erupted. Noise, which began within the center of my chest as the thumping of my pulsing blood, escalating toward an explosion. Noise, which left me as a collection of shattered pieces ricocheting across the winter night at deafening volumes, and whose sparks were extinguished when met by the icy ground. I became a shower of bullet casings, shot from somewhere deep inside, a part of me that violently objected to the spaces my mind wandered. But, the only evidence of the explosion was the cloud of warm breath as the smoke of shots fired, lingered in this cold icy air.

Dissociation.

I don't look like much of anything and that's a start. It's hard to find a blank slate, but when I look in the mirror I see nothing. My freckled face and pale white skin become a still hollow casing, which is holding up the illusion that I, too, am a person. No one is aware of the imposter I have become, of the zipper that starts at the base of my neck. This is a costume for my performance that condones me as you, and you, and you. I am just like all of you when walking down the crowded, bustling streets of this gray city, but simultaneously I am not. The zipper gives way to the truth that lies beneath this cracked and fragile façade, testifying that I am, in fact, a shattered, scared, bruised, and ugly mosaic of past experiences. Unzip this costume and there beneath my taped up, molded illusion of perfection lies a small, frozen child. Ice surrounds her, ice has become her, and to attempt to move her would be to risk shattering her into a million hollow pieces.

Nightmare.

When I hear the knocking on the door, soft and urgent, time stops and I am sucked into a whirlpool whose current pulls me into a dark, cold drain. Falling and falling, my stomach becomes a part of my throat, sitting where my esophagus meets my mouth, preventing my voice from calling out for help. I am gone, that much I know, because the sun is gone and the lights are turned off and my heavy eyelids have closed with the weight of a thousand bricks. Locked and loaded, my fingernails transform into ten long, sharp blades scratching at my chest at an attempt to penetrate my fragile soul. My body doesn't work, because my mind won't allow it. Prison; that is what the paralysis of sleep promises. Limp, helpless paralysis becomes a familiar presence. One, where circumstance is the fugitive and the night is the culprit.

02/25/16

Monday evening, I am in my class that centers around art practices in the community. For class this week, we read an article about a group of artists that did a collaborative project with the Bayside community out in California. In this particular area, there are three distinct ethnic groups which make up the population. In order to bring all these diverse individuals together, the team of artists centered their initial community art practice around food. For example, preparing beans in three ways that represented the ethnic backgrounds of the individuals and then telling stories reminiscent of food preparation in their households growing up. These scenarios led toward a discussion with my class about food's ability to bring the community together and build connections that previously were missing. I agreed with everything spoken about. In truth, food has a beautiful ability to foster connection. Sharing meals is a time for conversation and relationship building. But I also couldn't help but start uncomfortably shifting in my seat as the conversation left me feeling empty and sad knowing that this was not the case for myself the majority of the time.

Our class is partnering with a residential treatment facility for men and women struggling with addiction. We are going to make art together as a collective and at the end of a two month period, we will have a show displaying all of our work. Our class has been brainstorming about different ways to build connection among the group we are collaborating with, and this article brought up the great idea of having food be a part of the first portion of the group. The idea is to have snacks together as people arrive while checking in with an intention for the group. Everyone in the class seemed on board with the idea.

"It would be a good conversation starter." "Yeah, an ice breaker. Everyone loves talking about food." "Everyone loves food in general." "No one is going to be opposed to having snacks." "I think it will draw more people to the group."

And right there in the middle of the class discussion, I was sucked out of my chair and dropped into a clear cage posed as an animal on display, estranged and isolated. Because every head around me was nodding in agreement with the suggestions around food, the comfort of food, the excitement of food, and I wasn't. I was sad and angry and hurt and confused because I couldn't for the life of me understand how an entire room full of people would agree that food only held pleasant memories and pleasant experiences. Because, for me—the animal in the cage—food had been the reason for disconnection. If I had heard in treatment that a group was offering some unknown snack at the beginning of session, I wouldn't have gone. If a community was sharing memories centered around food growing up, I would fall silent. The reality is that even being in recovery and starting to gain some distance from my eating disorder, when the suggestion of adding an element of food to our group was tossed around, my mind immediately disagreed. *"No snacks, no snacks, no snacks!"* And though, I know no one could hear my thoughts, I felt the expression on my face and my inability to participate in the conversation any longer subjected me to the clear cage in the corner of the classroom.

In class on Monday, I instructed my body to nod when needed, agree when necessary, as if putting on a show would mean that the key to the clear cage would somehow magically fall into my hand and I could unlock myself and walk alongside everyone else. But it is moments like this— speaking about food as comforting and connection provoking—that I am slapped in the face with the reality that my mind does not operate like everyone else's. I am—and always will be—different, and I can lie to myself saying that I don't live in a clear cage, but that would be precisely what I just said, a lie. Because in truth, there are clear walls that keep me separate from other people. I have an eating disorder, and that means that I think differently, and things that are seemingly normal and true for other people just aren't inside my world. So I fall back on the conclusion that I am different and alone as I sink lower into my chair and fall silently away from my class, painting my expression blank, and praying no one will see through into the screaming conversation happening inside my mind.

This is a diagnosis I believe I should etch into my bones: *Terminally Unique*

It is soaked in a sea of irony. Though believing I am vastly different—so much so that I am walking around in a clear cage that forever keeps me from other people, that I am unable to relate or even communicate—isn't completely valid, but that is how my mind works. No matter what, it fights to be a single entity in a web of two hundred million. Forever alone. Forever different. Terminally unique.

The first time I walked into a treatment center and was met with dozens of individuals whose thoughts were similar to mine, I decided I wasn't anything like them. I didn't cry over cheese. I didn't obsess over my body. I didn't think I was worthless. I didn't hate myself and use a number on a scale to try and give some leverage to those thoughts. I didn't, I didn't, and yet deep down, I felt a part of myself becoming entangled in those dozens of men and women. This feeling of entanglement was precisely why I had to convince myself I wasn't like any of these people. I didn't have an eating disorder, because if I did then I was like them. If I did, then I, too, needed help. If I admitted that I also had these racing thoughts of self-doubts, insecurities, and fears then I wasn't my own. Suddenly, my little entity would be woven into the web of everyone else's whose minds are all screwed up.

Fast forward to Monday's class, and I wasn't like them either. I wasn't because I had an eating disorder. Because on Monday, I rewound to that moment in treatment, using this example for the reason for my separateness from my class. Different because I had an eating disorder. Then in treatment, I would fast forward to classroom and workplaces for examples that I didn't have an eating disorder, couldn't have an eating disorder, never had an eating disorder. In life, I slip back on my mental illness and in treatment I slip back on my normalcy—always fighting to disconnect and become alone in my experience, one way or another.

Bottom line is my eating disorder likes to lock me in this clear cage. My eating disorder likes to—and often succeeds in—convincing me that no one could possibly understand me, because I wasn't like anyone else, when in reality, the clear cage is translucent. It can be walked right through because it doesn't actually exist. And, if I were really honest with myself—it never did. Because no matter how messed up I may believe I am, no one is incapable of connecting with another person. It is in our very nature to connect. We are human, and humans need other humans. So even if the food conversations gave me anxiety on Monday, I can't possibly convince myself that I don't have one positive memory around a meal that I could use to connect with my class.

Terminally unique is not a thing. It never has been and never will be.

02/29/16

In the center of a dark and tangled forest of thorns and vines,
I have built a house in a meadow. The meadow is the only
place where the sun meets the ground. The grasses are thick
and strong. They dance under the shimmering golden light
at noon. The forest around the meadow is too thick to
navigate. Once you enter you will never get out. Ever. It is
proven. It is true. Everyone lives on the outskirts of the
forest. They look at it from afar, hearing it whine and moan,
sounds of the broken hearted, sounds of those who will
never escape.

I was born in the forest. I never saw the sun. The tops of the
trees whispered of it, though. Growing and growing. It was
a competition to absorb all the golden light. I loved the
stories of the trees, of sunshine and blue skies and fluffy
white clouds that changed with the wind. My skin was dry

and scaly. My eyes were glazed and ruined. My heart was cold and fluttery. I had been claimed and regurgitated by the forest. The trees told me there was more and I believed them.

When I sleep, I dream of the meadow. I dream of a space free from the towering treetops, a space where I, too, could feel and know the sun. The meadow is real for me, as real as the darkness was for the rabbits and snakes and birds. When I wake up, I talk about the meadow and everyone in the forest scoffs and turns the other way. I started hating being awake and started sleeping more and more. The more I slept, the more the meadow grew until it was full and lush and I could hide in the grasses and no one would ever find me.

03/04/16

Time and time again, I have compared my eating disorder to a rubber band.

Phase One: Fusing

Initially, I had no idea that there was a band wrapped around me. I didn't know that I could only move so far without being pulled back. I had no idea that dieting was leading to starvation, or that cheat days were leading to binging and purging. I had no idea that spending hours at the gym was not normal. I had no idea that over the course of several years, the eating disorder had come in the form this rubber band to restrain me, my life, and my future.

The day I first became aware of the band around my body, I was seventeen. Hunger had left me doubled over, retching in pain as I tried desperately to close my eyes and sleep. My mind screamed for me to get out of bed and eat something. My body begged me to drink more water to help ease the Charlie-horses in my legs. This was not uncommon during this time, but something about this night stuck with me, because lying there unable to sleep, I had the thought that I didn't want to do this anymore.

I didn't want to restrict. I didn't want to get up at 4:30 a.m. to work out. I wanted cereal in the morning and to sleep past the sunrise. I wanted to feel warm again, and not have to line my bed with four comforters. I was seventeen, and that night I desperately wanted to get out of bed and eat and drink and end this agony that I was living in, and yet I couldn't. Something inside of me held me down, told me not to move, told me that I wasn't allowed to because if I did, then everything I had worked toward—all the weight I had lost, all the calories I had purged, all the hours spent ruminating over my body and weight and diets—would have been wasted. If I got up that night, I would be a failure, and failure was not something I could deal with. Upon realizing the paralysis of adhering my body's needs, I rubbed my hands across my torso and felt for the first time the rubber band around my waist that was now fused to my skin with no hope of removal.

Phase Two: Stretching
The rubber band was so much more uncomfortable once I knew it was there. It was tight and irritating. It gave me rashes and left my waist feeling sore. You know when you wear a ponytail too long and when you take it off your hair hurts? Well, imagine never being able to take out the ponytail. You always have to wear something that is cutting off your circulation and doesn't allow you to bend certain ways. A rubber band is tight, restricting even the subtlest of movements. Once it is fused to your body you are limited, disabled, and cut off from the rest of the world because with a band constantly tearing into your skin it is hard to do anything else.

The rubber band got thicker over the years. It got so big that people started to notice it was there. That's how I ended up under the microscope, listening to a bunch of doctors and therapists and dieticians trying to help fix me. I was willing to spend my days in rooms lined with couches and eating premade meals, but then I was told that no one was going to remove the rubber band for me, and I couldn't help but lose all faith in the process. The rubber band had fused to my body over the years, leaving me dependent on it. My blood supply now ran through it. It was a muscle that helped me to think and walk. It was a part of me and the professionals told me that they couldn't just cut it off.

I didn't like that answer. So, I hooked one end of the rubber band to a pole and started running in the opposite direction, running and running and running away from the arena that the band had chained me in, in the direction that promised me recovery, the direction that promised freedom. I ran with one end hooked on a pole because I thought that if I stretched the band far enough, it would eventually snap.

The opposite happened. Instead of a snapped rubber band resulting in the freedom I longed for, I got so exhausted that I had to forfeit the race. I had to rest my feet, and the moment I sat down, the rubber band pulled me back to the starting point—to the place where one end was hooked on a pole. After all that running and effort and energy, I landed myself back in a room full of couches with premade meals and professionals telling me that they couldn't cut the rubber band off, that I couldn't run from it expecting it to snap in two.

I didn't believe them. I started running again. Running and running, until the rubber band could stretch no further, and I was wrenched right back. Back to the pole, back to the couch, back to the professionals. The rubber band was too thick to snap, too thick to outrun, and too fused to remove. I sat on the couch and raised my hands in surrender.

Phase Three: Walking

Though running away from the rubber band didn't work, it did stretch the band out. During those times where I was running away from the rubber band, I was fully onboard the recovery wagon and doing everything in my power to get rid of the eating disorder. The times when the rubber band pulled me back to the pole were my seasons of relapse and re-entering treatment.

This process was exhausting, a push and pull, a back and forth marathon of trying to find any way to get rid of the band. Some positives did come out of these seasons though, because they stretched out that band, which represents the eating disorder's malicious voice inside my head. After these seasons, the band fit like a loose pair of sweats, rather than tight skinny jeans.

Because the band was now loose, I felt as though I could take a step back and truly look at it. This was the key all along. Walking with the band and slowly finding ways to loosen its grip. That is what the dieticians and therapists and doctors were trying to tell me. They weren't saying that I would never be free of the rubber band. They were saying that I had to first accept the band before I could learn its weaknesses. The running away from it and the multiple attempts to snap it were valid, but ineffective. It was too much too quickly. I had to slowly pull away and discover ways to become less dependent on it. I needed to find other ways of coping with pain, and acquire other skills to help me distract from behaviors. I had to learn how to live without the band, to cut off the blood supply running through it, and eventually it would just shrivel away and die.

Phase Four: Unknown

I haven't gotten here yet. I think it is supposed to be the phase where the rubber band eventually falls off somewhere along my walk. Where the band no longer fits, where it's no longer used. I think it's the point I come to when I am no longer concerned with the band and how it feels, until one day, I realize that it is just…gone.

I don't know if I believe in this phase. I don't know if I think the rubber band will be gone, but I do know that I have heard people talk about losing their rubber bands. They don't know when or how or why exactly. They just know that one day, they woke up and realized it was gone. Perhaps one day I will wake up, rub my hands along my torso, and find no rubber band.

Perhaps, one day.

03/16/16

An ambulance passes at an ungodly volume, leaving my ears ringing and heart racing. I hate the sound of sirens, now even more than before, for their suggestion of death and air of panic or alarm. I have enough fear swimming through my bones these days.

Fear lives in my bones, now. The fear is densely solid, like ice or glass, and not liquid, so it may swim, like in the past, through my veins. It has seeped into my bones. It is a fear that leaves a cloud looming over my body, not raining, not separating, just lingering with a daunting presence, giving rise to surges of anxious energies in my chest. I am constantly anticipating the sudden downpour of acid rain on my sensitive skin.

The siren shifts from a distant wail to a distressing beeping as I gain conscious awareness into my actual surroundings. It's 5:00 a.m. and the noise was not an ambulance, but rather the feverous calls of another day. Wednesday. 5:00 a.m. The sky is still black, and my room stings my exposed feet and hands in its chilling March air. *I don't like it,* I tell myself. This uncertainty, this cloud, this cold air, and so I escape into my intrinsically wired mind, searching for an air of belonging.

Two days ago, the humidity held me in the present. The air's thick cloud offering a warm embrace certain to keep my feet—whose tendencies are to float away—firmly planted on the ground. The dry chill of the city lets me slip like water through loose fingers slowly spilling across the room.

I enter periods of time where I feel like everything is a dream, where it feels as if I am watching myself on a screen, sitting on the couch sipping black coffee in hopes that the bitterness will somehow transport me back into the scene. My complex mind needs this space, a time to rest from my existence, recharge, and reenter. This is also a time to disembark on a journey of wonder and fantasy, a time to create within myself a world separate from the one greeting me at 5:00 a.m. on a dark, cold Wednesday morning.

Somewhere wedged between the left and right side of my brain, I have carved a cubby and stashed my dreams there. So that whenever my presence becomes tangled and I am forced to cut myself free and float away, I can escape there. I can nestle in and unfold with the comfort of the ocean. That's what I stored within the cubby—a deep fascination and obsession with diving into a realm few get to experience. That's the recipe needed on these bleak disconnected days—a vivid imagination, one able to transport me from my cold bedroom to underneath the waves, carried by the current, and surrounded by sea life.

03/17/16

Sssshhhh. Silence is not quiet. Heavy reverberations of sonically charged weight ringing in my ears, leaving me worn, dry, and slowly unraveling.

My sanity is a ball of strings, loose noodles, boiled and left to dry out inside my skull. Silence cuts like a razor, dismantling, shredding the ball of yarn, and my sanity falls to the wayside, forgotten, misplaced, and irrelevant. It is now no more than chopped thread, or mutilated spaghetti, like a child chewing and spitting out my brains on a tray, reeking of vile, projectile vomit, and resembling my mind.

My god-damn complex mind.

03/30/16

Help me to escape my mind, which has transformed from a dormant mass to an electrical field of pulsating terrors. Whose electrical storms can't be predicted just as the shocks' damage can't be estimated.

Instead, the mass which takes up residency in my skull must be understood as a natural disaster to the utmost degree, a category five hurricane hovering near the coastline, a taunting force of destruction, and the source of the panic rising in my chest. It is not my mind that requires surgical removal, but my circumstances. Cut those out and bury them somewhere far beneath the ocean's stormy surface, that though necessary to regain my sanity, can't be done. Attempting to remove circumstance is to isolate body from time, the mind from thought, and those things can't be accomplished unless time didn't exist. And if time didn't exist then everything would fall stagnant, be paused, and frozen. To live is to be warm and without time I would be cold, an icicle in space, floating aimlessly with no footing in what we call *life*. Without the ability to remove circumstance and without the necessity of dissecting my mind, what then? Leave the billowing storm near the shore and prepare for an impending disaster while living today?

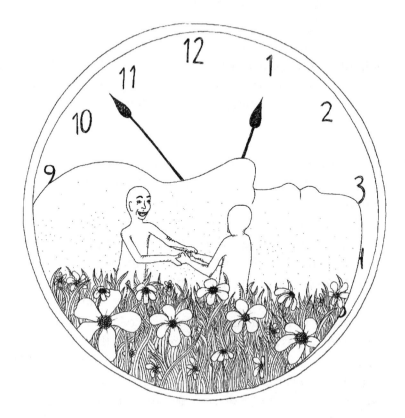

04/03/16

I have been escaping into the layers of my mind to find some resolution within my current circumstances. When I close my eyes, anything can become real if I envision it. So, I climb deep, deep down into a golden meadow, where I sit in the middle of a little brick house. Each brick laid by my own two hands. A safe house, built brick by brick to enclose the ones I hold dearest.

The meadow is vast and speckled with red flowers. Red is Andy's favorite color, and the flowers grow abundantly here. Taller and taller, until he and I and everyone else who

I want to protect are swallowed in their beauty. Hidden in their petals. Protected in their scent.

The sunlight dances, and the wind sings the meadow's melodies that change with the passing of time. But time here is not like time over there. In the meadow, time is never-ending. You do not have to be afraid of running out. Time is welcomed in the meadow. It, too, becomes an element of the choreographed dance of the sun and wind.

We dance, we sing, we laugh underneath the sun. Warmth radiates off of our cheeks, red and rosy they become, the beauty of the flowers reflecting back on us. We are not afraid. Here, we are never afraid.

When I open my eyes, the sharp sting of reality whips my cheeks as I take in the violent noise of my alarm. I am ejected from the world of safe havens built of brick houses and thrown into one in which time is limited. Time is ticking. Time is slowly running out. A world where the beeping of the alarm signals the panic to get up, get going, and get at another day. And there is no way for me to communicate with this reality about the world it is missing—the world that exists deep inside my mind.

I want that world, the world of eternity, the world where Andy is still alive, and where my mom is not sick with cancer, and I don't have an eating disorder, and Luke didn't find his brother under the car, and Laney wasn't crying herself to sleep, and Mary didn't have her mental breakdown, and survivors didn't exist. In the world of eternity, surviving wasn't real because all anyone knew how to do was live. I want my reality to erode like a rocky shore, let the waves cut at it—let it fall away, so that I may unravel into a place of perfection and safety. Take me to the meadow with the little brick house, where I can stick each person I love inside and build a room around them to ensure their safety. But that world is a myth. It is a byproduct of my overly imaginative mind. The world of dreams and perfection and wonder and magic. This world we live in is real, so real that it will stab you in the chest every so often just to make sure you feel it.

During the day I put on my mask. The mask has a screen over the eyes that places me in the meadow, and I wear it all the time because when I take it off, I don't know where I am or what day it is. When I take off the mask, I get really scared, and cold, and confused because I am suddenly thrust back in a world that I don't want to know. But that is the truth, isn't it? That the world cannot be known. Reality cannot be understood—especially when it entails the loss of someone so suddenly and so young. It will never be understood.

So what, now? Do I just take off the mask and stand naked in the world, with the cold and foreign winds freezing my tears to my raw cheeks? Do I wear the mask and live in a meadow, build up more bricks, dance in the wind and flirt with time until the sand in the timer runs dry, and the façade I spent so much energy building slowly disintegrates, and I am left as a shadow in a world full of solidity?

If I live with a mask on, I will fall away from what is true. The mask is what keeps me from the grief. It is the disconnect from the tragedy of losing Andy, and of the uncertainty of my mom's illness. Even if I choose to wear it, the grief will find me eventually, so I have taken it off and put it in the closet. It would be a disservice to Andy's memory to pretend he wasn't worth grieving over, but I need people to be patient with me for this very reason. I have taken off the mask, but I am standing in the cold winds, and I am sad, and angry, and hurting. The winds feel like knives cutting at every aspect of myself—the heart, the mind, the soul.

Some days, just simply breathing is all I can manage to do. Some days, I walk all the way to work and then can't make it in the door because I'm blinded by the waterfall of tears flooding from my eyes down my cheeks. Some days, I can't speak when I am in class because the kid across the room looks just like him. Other days, it is okay, it is bearable. The grief is able to walk alongside me instead of crushing me.

Without the mask, I am leaving behind the meadow and the dreams of eternity that live in it. I am leaving it behind not because I don't believe in heaven, but because I don't believe I am there yet. I am leaving it behind so I may look at this world—this reality, these circumstances—and begin to figure out how they are going to work with this crater that Andy's death has left behind.

Without the mask, my mind is much more vulnerable, much more exposed, and the grief is real. When grief is real, time is ruthless, and waves of emotion start to dictate my days, but I think that is acceptable. I think it is better to grieve than to stuff, and that riding the waves is important. I think that not making it work one day doesn't constitute as a failure and that letting myself be sad is good. Grief has a purpose, it reminds me how much Andy mattered.

04/10/16

My mind is shooting out words that don't exist, so my thoughts are unable to translate into anything outside of myself. That leaves me misinterpreted, a sheet of ice, but I am not translucent. I am black ice. I am opaque and dense and dark. I am as black as midnight, a mixing pot of anything and everything. I am dismantled and bonded paraxial pieces.

My words are gas and therefore, they don't exist as more than a passing inhale, digested, used, and then gone. My thoughts leave my existence clouded because they are chained to my goddamn mind. Through the debilitating power they have, my thoughts become real, and the alienated existence they possess—the gas they embody—suffocates my entire reality. Thoughts that they don't know, can't know, will never know because the words formulating them don't exist. Forever fostering a storm of intangibility, determining an inevitable madness within. Who wouldn't become mad if trapped inside themselves with only the compiling weight of words left unspoken for company? Words that can't be spoken, because they are created in the language of my mind—a language that only exists among my thoughts, one that I am unable to translate for them, because those words only make sense in the realm of my own reality.

Instead, I abandon the idea of the mind, thoughts, alienation, and the failure of these elements to actually exist. I look to melt my heart, my many hearts, the one in my chest, the one in my gut. Leg heart. Calf heart. Heart heart. A powerhouse control center for each pulsing activity that dictates my physical existence. My leg heart—frozen as all of my hearts are from a winter formed from years of manipulation, annihilation, culmination of false truths—must melt so that the pillars of solid ice can become water. They must be water if I am to move, to run, to dance, to swim in the form that once was my legs. If I were to move now, shattered shards of ice made from glass would crumble beneath the weight of my frozen body, and leave my face heart plastered against the hard pavement, the blood of my head heart pouring down the gray ground and steam forming to note the process of the rising temperatures. Warm pavement means the winter of past traumas is gone. As a result, it leaves a pool of red, leaking from my head heart's icy center. It splatters in a mosaic of painted glass surrounded by what was once two pillars—my legs, my statue legs, my frozen legs. It was the collapse of the hearts that began the melting that promised the future of spring.

But snow is still falling, and I find my mind swimming in the magic that exists inside each individual flake. Each flake is unique, complex, and different. Each with their own story, and yet together is when they start to become seen, formulating a blanket of white, which cloaks a dark and somber world. I walk in the snow, the flurries melting in my hair and hands. They are frozen, and I am not because I am warm and I melt them upon contact.

Maybe it is only within me that spring is beginning to arrive, because everything around me is still living in a never-ending winter. The snow paints me with wonder and incomprehensible excitement for the complexity of the one dropping the snowflakes. I look up with certainty that these flakes are for me, because I understand the language in which they fall. It is the language of the heavens, of the universe, of the other worlds. The ones of angels and demons, of God and Andy. The language not made up of words, that somehow makes sense of the unexplainable.

Pain, heartbreak, trauma, and illness make sense under the language of snow. The snow speaks of a collective beauty composed of individual artistic masterpieces. In the contrast of the white, even the darkest of experiences become stunningly beautiful. Suddenly, the words which my mind is shooting out—the ones that don't exist—I can become exceedingly grateful for. It is through my comprehension of the language of snow that I come to realize that I am living a four-dimensional existence in a three-dimensional world, and that is a magical thing.

04/12/16

Real Recovery

The Early Stages:
Finally laying my head down at night after successfully managing behaviors, only to find the eating disorder screaming about the feeling of my bloated stomach and swollen cheeks. Of my mind combating with, *"That is just the results of proper nutrition and hydration."* Of my eating disorder yelling back, *"How could you let yourself indulge in such glutinous acts? Tomorrow you have to get back on track. Tomorrow, or else you will just get fatter,"* while I peacefully drift off into a fragmented sleep dreaming of daisies and rainbows and how much I love this magical idea of recovery....

The Middle Stages:
Sitting at a restaurant blinking back tears at the fact that my thighs are touching. I am trying to hold a conversation while simultaneously panicking about the selections on the menu. I had wanted to challenge myself tonight. I'd planned to get something I truly wanted—pizza, pasta, burgers—thoughts of my favorite foods were so painfully alluring, leaving my mouth salivating. Now with my thighs touching, there seemed to be no way I could indulge in such delicacies. My friends and family could, the stranger next to me could, but not me. Never me. Poor me. Terminally unique me.

I had come to convince myself that I no longer had a problem: normal weight, eating the meal plan, minimal behaviors. But, I excuse myself to the bathroom to cry silently about how badly I wanted the taste the bread in the bread basket but couldn't find the strength in my sausage arms to reach it, I realized the problem was still there. Loud.

Obnoxious. I started to wonder if recovery was all just some big lie fed to me by treatment centers to simply steal my money.

I didn't get the bread, and I didn't order what I truly wanted, and the disorder applauded me the whole walk home while I beat myself up for listening to it.

The Relapse Stages:
These came interspersed. I would be good for a while, and then my disordered friend would steal the driver's seat. Either through a new behavior or a new mindset, he kept coming back, relentless and leaving me in what felt like an endless cycle of *getting better* and then *getting worse*. It was banging my head against a wall, chasing my own tail, redefining insanity as I reached for the same deadly comforts over and over again.

The Done Stages:
I got really good at bullshit during my time in treatment centers. The bullshit came at times when I was there but didn't want to be there. It left me feeling stuck, trapped inside the treatment centers walls, and surrounded by dozens of disorders just like mine. I didn't want the constant reminder of my disease mirrored in each individual to my left and right. It wasn't helpful. In fact, from other eating disorders, I learned all kinds of tricks to keep me sick. I played the game just like so many others. The game I am not actually playing at all, but instead my eating disorder is kicking goals and shooting hoops all for the wrong teams while I sit back and slowly disappear into the recesses of my mind.

The Awakening Stages:

I came to believe that a power greater than myself could restore me to sanity.

Realizing the magnitude of the disease inside my mind, resulted in me falling deeply and madly in love with the idea of a Higher Power. Someone to help the helpless little bird I had become, someone to love me when I hated every inch of my existence, someone bigger than the eating disorder who could help me get away from it.

God met me when I was willing to meet them—when I asked for help, truly asked. Not the prayer where my fists still desperately clenched onto my eating disorder as I prayed for help, but the *fall on my face, arms opened wide, help me I am broken* prayer. That is the one that God heard and suddenly, I began to believe in this recovery that everyone was talking about. The voice of God—of hope, of surrender—was louder than the manipulative, abusive, narcissistic disorder inside my mind.

The Real Stages:

Each day is impossible, filled with the highest of highs and the lowest of lows. When the disorder was truly given up, I felt everything. Even after the awakening which unleashed the desire for recovery, I still had to return to the basics. Baby steps. Take your time. Relearn yourself.

I have a meal plan. I have a treatment team. I go to EDA. I eat, I sleep, I pray, I cry, I write, I make art, and I talk. But above all, I think about concepts larger than calories, food, and the circumference of my thighs. Most days, that is. Remember, nothing is perfect.

I am slowly coming undone, collapsing into a new alignment of the broken pieces I have been composed of. I am transforming. I am in so much pain awaiting the beauty that is being created. And that is recovery—pain, change, gain, repeat.

04/22/16

there's something oddly upsetting
about the emptiness in the moments between
i don't know where to put my hands
or place my thoughts
i no longer know how to be because there are no numbers
instructing me

it's the moment when you're waiting for the internet
browser to open
or the dryer to finish
the train to come
the coffee order to be called
when i reach for my phone
anxiously scrolling through a million images i never needed
to see
i become fixed
somewhere to be
somewhere to focus
but what if i am focusing all wrong

i want to learn how to be bored
i want to remember how to just sit
the disease took that from me
took away patience
took away calm
i want it back
i sit and stare and fight the urge to do anything more

05/12/16

Living with an eating disorder is like waking up every morning and putting on a costume. I am surrounded by messages that lead me to believe that unless I am frail, bony, or medically compromised, I can't struggle. If I am smiling and positive, then I can't say I am in emotional pain. The costume morphs me into an image accepted by society, keeps me in line with what I need to be. Society is filled with ignorance surrounding what an eating disorder truly looks like. That's why living in recovery requires taking away my presentation and showing others what these diseases are capable of.

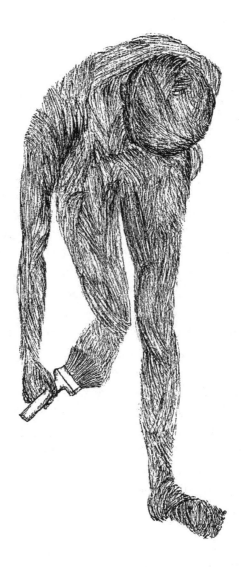

05/20/16

I matter because I exist. I may never fit in. My experience sticks out because where everyone else is painted white, I am blue.

06/04/16

To the woman at the gym:

I see a piece of me in you. At first glance my eating disorder tells me we are the same, but it is just a piece, a part, one parasite that has infected both you and me, me and you and, by unfortunate statistics, many others.

Your eyes are like an animal, digesting the numbers flashing in front you. Fierce. Determined. Hungry for something bigger than what that treadmill is going to give you. But there you are, eating the wrong sustenance, burning off what little fuel your body is craving. Next to me, right there, I could reach out and turn off the machine. I could turn off the obsession. I could save your screaming legs. I could end it. But I can't, and I know that. Turning off the machine won't turn off the thoughts for you.

Only you can save you from the beast inside your mind. Only you can decide to become friends with your body. Only you can start the fight, not the machine, because that is not the enemy. But fight the illness in your mind that tells you to keep on going. Keep going toward what? Death? Illness? An eating disorder? An exercise addiction? Do you even know the fire you are playing with?

I can't exercise next to you. Your machine is infecting my mind as well. We are not the same. My mind tells me we are, but I know we aren't because I am going to move. I am leaving. I am going home to a dinner and shower and rest. I am different because I know that you are playing a game that can't be won and I am not playing anymore.

06/05/16

You deserve to take up a damn whole lot of space.

06/23/16

"The body is a machine. You must use it or it gets rusty."

I came across this line written in one of my journals from 10 years ago. When I wrote this, I was eleven years old and referring to my body in relation to dance. Writing about how to improve myself as a dancer, I would first have to build the machinery of my body. Strengthen the legs, improve flexibility, stamina, concentration, etc., all things that to become a dancer—which at the time was all I wanted—are necessary. But what does it mean for my body to be a machine when I have an eating disorder? Because I can tell you when I wrote those words at eleven, I wasn't thinking in terms of fascination with my body's abilities. I was writing from a place of resentment with my body's inabilities. I wanted to be better, stronger, faster, and thinner. I wanted everything that my body was not giving me.

When my eating disorder began, I had very little knowledge about what was happening. I didn't realize that with every minute spent obsessing about food or challenging myself to shrink a little farther, I was feeding a parasite inside my mind. I was allowing it to grow and grow and grow until it had swallowed any rational thoughts around body image, food, exercise, and my self-worth. But how was I supposed to know, when I didn't realize there was a parasite overtaking the mechanics of my body?

After the parasite swallowed my mind, it had control of my body—with its only goal being to destroy its operation. Not all at once, no big explosion, or anything like that. That would be far too simple, and the parasite likes slow and painful downfalls, to shut it down gradually. Forget to charge it, forget to oil it, unscrew the bolt needed to connect the stomach to the heart or the heart to the mind. Allow the deconstruction to take time, to take effort, to happen so gradually that I—the person the parasite has invaded—am unaware of its reign.

Then there came a day when I realized something was not quite right. When I got up in the morning, my arms didn't quite work, and my head was spinning. My legs were like lead and my stomach was in a constant knot. I went to charge my machine—my body, my life source—and found that I couldn't reach my arms to grab the cereal for breakfast, or even the phone to call for support. I found that I was not in control, and I started to hear the voices in my head—the malicious banter of the parasite sitting in the control room of my mind. *"Don't eat that." "Go running, even though you feel tired." "If you eat that, you will have to eat all of that." "If you touch that, you will grow rapidly and never stop." "Do this, do that, do this, do that."*

But something strange happened once I became aware of the parasite. With awareness came a desire to push back, to restrain myself against the parasite's demands. No one wants to be under the control of someone, or something else. I wanted my machine back in working order. I just couldn't do it alone. So I called in some troops, professionals who had seen other parasites like the one inhabiting my body, and I let them start the excavation process, to dig as much as they could out of my mind.

All of that was good. All of that made sense. The development of an eating disorder, the realization you need help, and the journey through treatment has been talked about a thousand times over. But what happens after the professionals help you excavate the parasite? What happens when you are sent back out into a world with a newly discovered mind but a machine—or body—that no longer responds to your voice? What happens when you have spent years and years under the reign and direction of something else, and now suddenly you are expected to be the controller of your own machinery?

This is the point in the recovery journey that I personally found the most challenging. I felt the most lost, the most confused, and the most misunderstood. Here I was— someone whose entire existence had been shaped for the past decade or so by a disease inside my mind, who had put their life on hold for a long time to enter into treatment, to get help, to start healing—leaving and rejoining the real world with no knowledge of what my world *should* look like. I didn't know myself, my body, my soul, or my spirit. I had left school and work, switched majors, lost friends, and lost my coping mechanisms. I was out. I was *in recovery*, with absolutely no idea of how to navigate or sustain it. All I knew was my eating disorder and now, by the grace of treatment, I knew it backwards and forwards. I knew my fear foods, new coping skills, and what emotions I had suppressed. I knew eating disorders and could have written an entire book on what mine looked like alone. What I didn't know was my machine—I didn't know myself. I didn't know my body, and treatment did not help me to figure that out.

Figuring out the body's machinery after years of it being controlled by the parasite of an eating disorder has been the most rewarding and simultaneously painful experience I have ever endured. It is the part of the recovery journey that I am most passionate about—the part where you stop relearning the eating disorder. You stop counting exchanges, and managing weights, you stop obsessively talking about how the eating disorder snuck into your week, or how you failed to cope well on Saturday night. Though, all those things are needed in recovery as well, but what I am speaking to is the necessity of pairing them with meaning—pairing those nitpicky logistical aspects of eating disorder recovery with how to connect with the world again. How to wake up in the morning and be able to know that you have a larger purpose than what you are going to have for breakfast, or how far you will run at the gym. To know that you are in control of that machine you live in, that it is charged, and oiled, and ready to take you wherever you desire to go. This is recovery. Recovery is about passion. It is about moving past simply maintaining the body's machine and finding a sense of normalcy around maintaining health, food, weight, and exercise so that you can quiet yourself enough to hear the slow, constant hum of the soul. The soul only sings when the machine is running, when it is in order—updated, waxed, and shined. When the body is healthy, then the soul is present.

What fills the soul is the most important aspect of sustaining recovery. Until I found things to fill mine, I could never remain in recovery. Instead I would go to treatment, *heal* the body, talk of coping skills, leave, and relapse—over and over again, until one day I stopped long enough to see that this doesn't work, that the healing of the body without taking time to listen to the soul will only reap destruction. Destruction is all I knew. The parasite taught me how to deconstruct the machine, and so when I would leave treatment and become the director of my body again, that is what I would fall back on. Destruction.

I don't blame myself because I didn't know any better, but if I were to have taken a minute to listen to the soul, it would have been there all along—quiet for many years, but always there. It would have been singing those times I left treatment about the ocean, and art, and writing, and traveling. It would have been giving me a meaning for sustaining my body's machinery. I just didn't know I was supposed to be listening.

So, what is it like to see my body as a machine? Fascinating. Breathtaking. Stunning. To think that the heart works with the brain, and the brain with the lungs, and the lungs with the throat, and the throat with the stomach. It is a dance, a dance to the song of the soul who sings constantly to the rhythm of the machine's hum. My blood is always pumping without my knowledge of it. My brain is always sending out electric currents without me realizing it. My body is a complex array of systems that together give me the ability to write, dance, dive, wake up in the morning, smile, laugh. It is the soul that gives me butterflies in my stomach when I think about my spirituality, or the deep belly laughter when I think about those I love, or the overwhelming longing when I think about the ones I have lost. I found the soul in the ocean when I went scuba diving. I found one place where the parasite, or the eating disorder, had never been before. I figured out that the parasite couldn't swim, and that beneath the surface I could see life through a new lens. I found the soul in writing, in words given to those struggling with eating disorders, through connecting with others and offering them streams of hope. The soul lives in my faith, in my Higher Power, in all of the things that give me a sense of passion, purpose, and meaning. The soul is the feeler: the body is the doer. Unless they work together, nothing will actually be achieved in recovery.

This is my constant encouragement for those struggling with eating disorder recovery: to lean on the things that make you feel something. Lean on something positive. It doesn't have to be anything huge, like scuba diving. It could simply be the fact that you think flowers are beautiful, so you buy a flower or go to a park and sit next to some flowers. Think about why it is they look beautiful to you, and then hold onto that for your recovery. Apply some beauty into your thoughts, actions, and intentions, and see where that takes your recovery for the day. Continue this. Do it every day until listening to the soul is routine, until the soul is in line with the machine you are learning to control and direct without the rule of the parasite inside your mind.

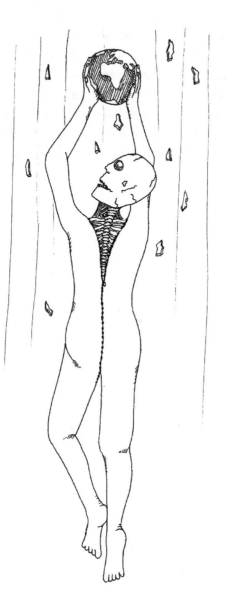

07/12/16

unzip my spine

peel back my skin
unhinge my soul
give me freedom or give me death
because i don't want to live between them anymore

* * *

07/15/16

the world is small
i am gigantic
i hold it in my hand
i crush it with my heel

* * *

07/20/16

the moment a slip becomes a fall
and momentum rules your life
speed becomes a drug
while bottoms dissolve to dust

* * *

07/22/16

tears of glass slice through to bone
etching caves beneath the nose
where teeth may grow and lips speak words
until air breathes as fine as snow

08/25/16

i was four the first time i was called ugly

i was six the first time i went on a diet

i was seven the first time i was told i have thunder thighs

i was nine the first time i was called freckle face

i was eleven the first time my body fell apart

i was fourteen the first time i prayed that i would die

i was sixteen the first time i made myself throw up

after that i was gone

i lit myself on fire

i didn't mean to but it felt like a natural progression of events

11/17/16

loss is...

loss is my unblinking eyes watching the clock turn from 3:02
to 3:03 a.m.
the shadow left on the closet door from the street light across
the alley
the distant sound of the train *dadafabba dadafabba*

loss is the moment before the train doors open at my stop
the anxiety and preparation before darting off onto the
platform
to be swallowed on the staircase by dozens of professionals
who have an appetite for lethargy

loss is the shoelace that won't stay tied
the water bottle that leaks all over my backpack
the scratched credit card when all I wanted was a large
coffee
only to have the coffee I fought to buy burn my already
swollen tongue
loss is the hangnail on my thumb
loss is the knot in my neck
my creaky hip
my itchy eyes
the cystic zit on the tip of my chin

loss is the space between 3:03 and 3:04 a.m. when nothing
makes sense and everything feels frozen
where suddenly i am writing about a hangnail i don't have
and a shadow that doesn't exist
while listening to the hum of the train
and wondering if his ghost is its passenger tonight

11/20/16

one two three four
my footsteps cut craters through the cement floor
in the shape of unexpected death
swirly smoky vortex of death
voices on the street get caught in the black
black like tar sticky like tar tar like pupils
staring downwards into a sea of nothing
when i scream into the crater
my voice fights back slicing my tongue in two
leaving me mute leaving me bleeding
bleeding red into smoke
liquid drops swallow the gas
becoming a black and red tar of stolen pasts
so i stop and sink as my legs melt to tar
tar that sticks sticks that break like twigs

twigs are thin and fragile

fragile like my pupils pupils too weak to watch
as my unmovable feet melt my limbs down to bone
and i sway in the wind of passing bodies i don't know
one two three four
broken twigs fall to craters burned in the cement floor

12/15/16

Loss is the reality of never being able to hold someone again, to have a conversation with them, or simply hear them say your name. There is a hollowness, an unexplainable emptiness that fills the space in your chest that I didn't understand until Andy disappeared.

12/16/16

i saw a limping deer and my mom's legs are weak
everything feels heavy while my chest is turning to ice
my heart is shattered like the falling autumn leaves
but no one noticed because i have paper clipped my lips up
permanent happiness without attainable joy
like a limping deer i close my eyes
and pray for the disintegration of my thunder thighs

12/17/16

what happens when you're a recovery advocate for over
10000 people and you relapse
not slip not lapse but relapse
what do you do
how do you admit to fucking up
to falling on your face again
i don't know
who do i ask that would know
many times i feel like giving up
i don't because that would be selfish
but more than anything i want it all to stop
i'm just so tired

12/18/16

I do this thing on nights when I want to disappear. I send people messages reminding them how much they matter, an encounter that I had with someone that changed me, or words they said that lifted my spirits. It's an impulse, naturally responding to my feelings of worthlessness.

I want others to feel worth something, because I know what it feels like to have that horrible silence. The silence that falls over your soul when your mind's darkness freezes it. I know what it's like to lie on your couch for seven hours straight doing nothing, simply because your brain has given up. It hurts too much, living, but you think dying would be selfish so instead, you just dream of falling away and send messages to others in an attempt to keep them from doing the same.

2017: *an unfortunate series of relapses, not the slow crawl I had experienced in the past but a huge leap back into my eating disorder, a forced admittance of being too scared of the world without the structure of numbers to fall back on, ending with a deep conviction that it was time to finally be done with being a slave to my eating disorder's wishes*

01/15/17

Life felt too full and rich, and I became too much again—so I relapsed for the third time, falling deep deep down underwater, where I could no longer hear all the noise. People still laughed and danced, and I was there, but I was distant. A hundred feet below, a murky shadow in their memories, and only an impression of my own reflection. I was no longer me—the eating disorder made sure of that. I was first and foremost the love child of anorexia and bulimia, left only to act according to their will. I wasn't exactly sure why—or how—I got to this place, but some demons inside my head dragged me lower than any previous low weight, larger than any binge, more aggressive than any purge. In January of 2017, I was sitting on the beaches of Tanzania amongst my art therapy class, dancing and singing with Tanzanian artists—but dead inside. Completely dead. Not a single beat of the drums spoke to my heart, or rattled my bones, or flowed through my veins. Steady silence ruled my existence, and a misleading smile painted my face. To the class and the artists, I was calm, peaceful, a steady presence—but inside was a war I had forfeited. Slowly I was dying, but this death wasn't seen because it was dressed behind a pleasant girl in a flowered dress.

Somewhere between the second relapse into bulimia in 2015 and this current relapse (which seemed to be the lethal combination of the two diseases: anorexia and bulimia) my mom understood that I needed her. I was grown and yet, I felt like a child fighting a giant. My mom was beginning to see this illness for what it was: a killer. She saw the heaviness in my eyes, felt the coldness of my finger-tips. She saw it steal my passion and love, when before I made her turn the other way, putting on a show so she wouldn't have to see me collapse behind my mask. She watched as her daughter slowly was eaten by this monstrous disease, and she was there to support. Her support was built on this new fear that the disease might actually take me—kill me, bury me—and she would have to watch. For the first time, I let her hear the doctors' concerns, and the whispers of my own insecurities. As a result, I found I was leaning more on her than on myself. I had lost all faith in my ability to win this battle— my mom, my family, my friends—they were all I had left. Perhaps they could pull me out.

The weeks leading up to Africa, I had felt different than ever before, like I was watching myself in a movie. I would see images in my mind of a happy, full Morgan, singing, dancing, and running around. I would hear music and feel warmth, see bright colors, and speak with confidence. Then I would snap back, someone would say my name, or my head would fall back, and I would come to realize the truth. I was a cold, starving child.

I had convinced myself that these images that were coming to my mind were God's way of bringing my dying body peace. I didn't think it was a picture of the future, but perhaps how I would appear once I was in heaven, once my body gave up after these years of abuse. But this idea scared me, dying. Not because I am scared of dying—no, I would love to die because I am too tired to fight anymore. Instead, I am scared of who would hurt when I was gone.

I think of Andy and how much agony I feel about his absence. I don't want my family to go through that pain again. I think of Andy's laugh and spirit a lot, wondering why God took him and not me—who was so quiet, scared, weak, unnoticed. I think about how different things would be if the roles were reversed. Andy deserved life. He was in

love with it, cherished it. He embraced it, while I fight life—
in a constant war between the light and dark. His peaceful
presence would have impacted more people than mine, but
here I am—stuck and drowning. Praying over and over
again in my Tanzanian hotel room, "*God, give me energy and
strength to make it back home.*"

Tonight is a full moon, and perhaps that will bring me peace
as I fall into my dreams—peace of mind and peace of body.

01/30/17

I admitted to residential for the third time, and had to take a leave of absence during my last semester of college. I met the dietitian, but I didn't trust her. The psychiatrist was awkward, the nurse was weird, the doctor was irritating, and my therapist scared me. I am a pessimist: what can I say? I think life is a hopeless mess. Well, not everyone's life...mainly just mine.

01/31/17

I didn't sleep last night. Leg cramps, a crazed heart, and my unsettled mind made it impossible to calm down. There was a bright, blaring exit sign in the corner by my bed that blinked red whenever I shut my eyes, and the nurse kept coming in every half hour.

I don't understand how I fell this far. How did I end up back here? I tried to remember, but everything is blurry and hard right now. My throat screams for water. I don't know why my mind won't allow my body the simplest of needs.

02/04/17

The world is a sticky place, full of messy people, and messy situations. There's nothing we can guarantee ourselves, because nothing is promised. But I do know that there are things larger than myself, things beyond what I can see and hear. They exist when I breathe air into my lungs, or hear my sister laugh. I feel it in my chest when I am holding someone I love. I know the three dimensions in which I understand the world are small in comparison to the spiritual realm that exists. Death and loss helped me to understand this on a deeper level. Andy, though not here physically, will always exist within my spirit. Forever and always, he will be the person I look forward to reconnecting with someday. He believed in me, and since his life was cut short, I must continue mine in his honor.

02/20/17

Icicles swim through my lips, straight down my throat, taking up residency in my hollowed lungs. They are sharp, like crystal, and make it impossible to breathe. There's no room for air in my frozen chest. Memories are like heat. They come and melt the frozen chest, leaking shards of crystal glass through all the parts of my body. It's painful. The glass cuts everything in its path, but it won't last. The body has an amazing way of discharging everything it doesn't need. And so I stand and breathe in deeply, allowing the storm of flashbacks to pass through my bloodstream and across my eyelids.

"Images are more vivid when your eyes are closed. Can you open your eyes, Morgan?"

I hear the voice echoing somewhere in the distance, rebounding off the walls as if I were in a steel tunnel. One eyelid and then the other, I crawl my way back. It's a daunting task, taking every bit of strength my shattered body can muster.

"That's it. Now, can you make eye contact with me?"

I don't see anything. I can't even nod. I am suddenly so tired as if I have lived the weight of a hundred lives. My eyelids hang heavy, fluttering down and up. The memories flash here and then gone. A cup of ice is shoved into my hands— its temperature is jarring. It reminds me of my frozen lungs.

"I am in so much pain," I whisper to the counselor.

"Should I get the nurse?" the counselor asks.

I shake my head, slowly and carefully. She didn't get it—this pain wasn't something anyone could take away. This pain was imprinted on the memories of my mind.

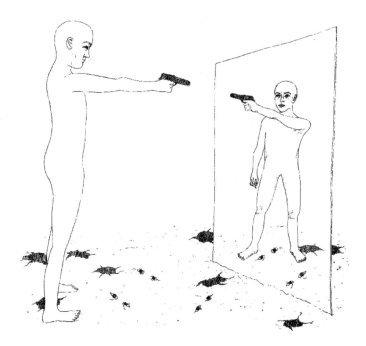

03/12/17

It's like walking through a minefield after the battle is all said and done. The guns have stopped firing, the cannons have all been shot, and only you are left standing. As you begin to walk around, you come to the realization that each casualty is staring back at you with a familiar face. There are dozens of pairs, glazed over, crystalized, frozen staring into a warzone aftermath. Only after surveying face after face, do you come to the startling realization that you had been aiming at yourself this entire time. Each pair of eyes staring up at you was a pair of your own. But, if they were all dead and they were all replicas of you, then how was it that you were still standing? The *you* is me, and this me is left untouched.

We can live a million lives, be shot down a hundred times, and still walk out of the war unscathed, because no human weapon can kill a soul. The soul will always remain your own because it is guarded by the very hand of God.

03/19/17

Don't humor the possibility of negative outcomes.

* * *

04/21/17

There's more to life than the here and now.

* * *

05/01/17

This is not the end of my story. That is why so many of my prayers seem unanswered.

* * *

05/06/17

Pain has become the fuel for my passion.

* * *

05/10/17

Love can't be learned in isolation. I have to be around people.

05/20/17

We are all called to belong, not just to believe in a belonging.

* * *

06/08/17

Stop grave sucking—let the old Morgan die.

* * *

08/23/17

"If we do not transform our pain, we will most assuredly transmit it."
-Richard Rohr

* * *

09/15/17

Hey God,

I really need your help.

* * *

09/18/17

I am chewing on a starburst, contemplating my entire existence while simultaneously spewing glitter, paint, and dirty water onto a canvas. I'm angry, I'm hurt, I'm terribly depressed, but I am smiling. Smiling because, at this point, who gives a fuck? After so many years of fighting, shouldn't I feel some kind of release by now?

* * *

09/24/17

The world becomes a lot less scary when you have someone who is slaying demons alongside you.

* * *

11/07/17

Air swims down the tunnel between my teeth and diaphragm with piercing tangibility. Pebbles—the air is pebbles, and their edges are sharp. I'm cut deep, and breathing suddenly becomes lethal. Blood, bleeding, memories of times stolen by such an insidious disease. Take my hands and crush my throat. Then, help me stitch it back together, because I need a body that is my own. I need a body that I own.

* * *

11/23/17

If my eyes were the sun, then would you quit looking through them as if they were glass?

11/30/17

The darkness bleeds through me like a toxic wasteland, unable to be contained. It's like trying to hold water with wide spread fingers, or hugging air. It escapes you, but the action consumes you. Leaning left and right, a disorientation where up becomes down, and down becomes up. What else can be done when your world is completely blinded by an overwhelming darkness that even shadows can't ignore?

12/28/17

The world is large and dynamic, scary and unpredictable. It's a breeding ground of spontaneous endeavors and unexplainable circumstances. Trying to understand is like driving in a fog—dangerous and disorienting. When I was young, I believed in magic and fairies—butterflies circled my thoughts and rainbows danced from my heels.

Time came and zapped electricity through my veins, leaving me uncomfortable and raw. Time became a viscous friend with whom I came to know too well. With years came anxieties; with anxieties came terrifying situations. Slowly the rainbows dissolved to dark clouds of lightning and unwanted electricity, and the butterflies turned to moths, attacking, biting. All the energies became green and luminous, haunting and scary. The world transformed from large and dynamic to small and predictable. My eyesight turned black, but for some reason, I stayed. It was an interesting warm. It was hauntingly familiar. It was my home entangled in this mess of unknowns. Loss, loss of the home—a series of losses initiated by the electricity of my touch. Loss was home, and home was nestled somewhere deep behind my eyelids. My heart swam through my chest, upwards to my pupils—pumping, thumping, reminding me that I am, in fact, alive.

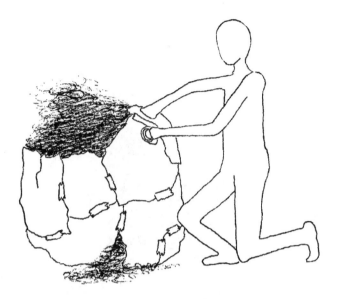

2018: *the year of commitment, the year of no turning back, the year of fighting each day for recovery while falling into bed exhausted yet satisfied for not giving into destruction, the year of rebuilding the life mental illness had destroyed*

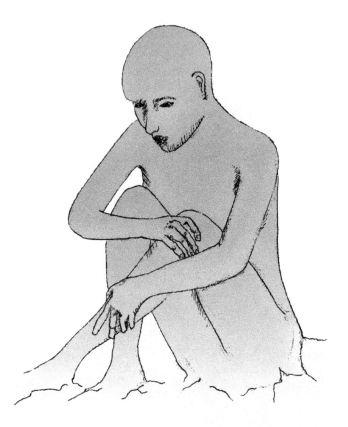

04/20/18

She's exhausted, but closing her eyes only makes it worse—
the images, the flashes, the pain in her stomach. *I am not safe,
I am not safe, I am not safe*—the words taunt her, playing over
and over again inside her brain. Who is she, but a fucked up
little girl who had everything taken and nothing given? She,
who is but a collections of bricks, weighed down and

unmovable no matter what the effort. Shatter her, drill out the facade—within is a child, a child so lonely and afraid. She wishes for nothing more than amnesia.

The memories—they won't go away, and they are debilitating. She sees the faces everywhere she goes, and feels it whenever she lies in bed at night. Her body is not hers. Her body is someone else's. There's nothing left but bricks for her to hold in place of a beating heart. *Thump, thump, thump*—the sound of each one slowly falling to the floor. They are too heavy to be held up—each one holding a separate memory, a hurt, a pain, a horrible time when nothing was okay. Nothing is okay. She knows this, but no one will believe her. She's happy, she truly is—but she's miserable at the same time. Chiseled into stone and created from the rubble, is a girl. A girl made of stone, everything is fake and hard. If her heart is also made of stone, how can she really be alive in the first place?

Leave her be and watch her slowly die while living. Second by second, becoming more like a statue, but no one can see that she's breaking—she's cracking. She cracks at night, and the mud and gore come spilling out, congealing beneath her onyx feet. There is the hatred, the open wounds, the unrelenting need for bandaging. She's bleeding out, but she never will, because she's made of stone, and stones don't bleed. No one can save her but herself, all on her own. *Her own her own her own*—these words hold the power of change, but what if nothing changes and everything remains the same? What if life is nothing but an illusion of segments sewn together?

05/02/18

I got lost somewhere between my twisting stomach and the darkness of my bedroom. I sank deep within myself, becoming as small as I possibly could. *Not real, not real, not real....* but it was. Memories, all these memories flash behind a thin layer of skin covering my pupils. This strange phenomenon that keeps me from sanity, the mind with its random moments of recollection and anxiety. I pull at my hair. I scratch at my cheeks. I feel them across my body. I am not my own. I am never alone. Curl up tighter, clench my eyelids harder, breathe, breathe, I have forgotten how to breathe. Violation clouds my every thought. The space between my legs throbs. My cheeks are damp with tears. I pray that I fall asleep soon in hopes that my dreams won't be haunted by the same thoughts. One, two, three—I count in times like these, times when I return to being ten or eleven or twelve all the way up to seventeen. I count and pray, and eventually time passes and my mind stops tormenting me, and I can find enough breath to be able to go about my night. But the evidence of my shaking hands keeps me from forgetting the dark shadows I am hiding from.

And I do go about my night, cooking and cleaning, and doing normal people things—all while wondering if I was in any way normal, anymore. After all the destruction—all the parts of me taken, all the bruises and blood and screams—how could I be anything anymore? I sometimes think that I am no longer human, but rather a strange mosaic of other people's experiences, fragments of their eyes, nails, voice, legs.

I crawl into the bathroom, turn on the shower to drown the noise of my sobs. Sob and sob and sob, for hours until I am all dried up and have nothing left to give the world. Then, I close my eyes and think about death—that's what my messed up soul does when life is too much—it dreams of dying, the sweet release of it all coming to an end.

08/10/18

My alarm goes off at 6:00 a.m. I have had to get up early every day, and I'm not sure why. It just seems like there is so much to get done, but I am not sure there really is anything that needs to be done. It's an anxious energy — a shaking hands and pounding chest kind of energy that leaves me lying in bed with racing thoughts and an inability to sleep. I took a sleep aid and two melatonin last night. I had worked hard to calm myself enough the last couple of months to ditch the sleep medication, but over the last week or so that has all fallen by the wayside as I let the pills slide down my throat.

I hit snooze. I worked until 10:30 p.m. last night, and didn't fall into bed until midnight, and the sleep aid was making it hard to open my eyes. *I'll just sleep a little longer*, I tell myself as I silently run through all the things that needed to be completed this morning.

Breakfast, devotional, clean, laundry, art project, workout, emails, Instagram post for UJ, don't forget to work out — it's really important you work out this morning – leave by 11:30 a.m. to meet boyfriend…

And I sleep a little longer, and a little longer, and a little…I jump out of bed. It's 8:30 a.m.! How did I sleep so long? I will never get everything done. I become a scurrying hamster, running around the apartment. Breakfast was rushed and I hate rushing meals. It makes me nervous, like I am doing something wrong. Food needs to be thought out and eaten slowly to ensure I am not overeating. What if I overate? But there was no time to humor that thought. Emails and emails and more emails. They are never-ending when you are planning trips, working at a treatment center, communicating about yoga jobs, and keeping up with UJ. Then I get distracted, my recovery voice comes in, and I take a deep breath. I remind myself that everything will get done in due time, that worrying will only make my day harder, that working out is not a top priority in my life anymore. I thank that voice. It is getting stronger these days, but there are still mornings, nights, or afternoons where it gets trampled by my demons.

Reminded of the peace that comes with recovery, I leave my room and sit on the couch next to my sister. I take some deep breaths, chat with her, and relax. Recovery is the sweet state of simply being. The morning proceeds. I shower, clean, and pack up some snacks for the day. I don't work out like I originally planned. I didn't have time, and I didn't want to strengthen those disordered voices in my head. Humoring them just wasn't worth my time anymore.

By the time I hop on the train at 11:30 a.m., I feel exhausted. I had fought several battles in the last couple of hours. I pat myself on the back. I look around me and find each passenger on their phones with downturned lips. It's hard silently fighting your head. There's no audience there to applaud you when you take your final bow.

08/14/18

My alarm went off at 7:00 a.m. I was supposed to leave at 9:00, but I didn't wake up until 9:25. I don't know why I am oversleeping every day this week. When I was in my eating disorder, I would be lucky if I slept past 6:00 a.m. I was always restless, agitated, and running around doing a million things, because doing everything was far better than sitting with my own thoughts. But here I am—staying up late, with enough energy to talk, watch movies, read, and write. I am beginning to feel like a normal human—what a weird and foreign concept to someone in recovery.

I was late, so I grabbed a protein bar, a granola bar, and water to eat/drink in the car. I had some coffee with cream and sugar—a new recovery phenomenon for me. At noon, I was asked if I wanted to go grab pizza. I panicked. In my disordered mind, I hadn't had any food that had any nutritional value. This, of course, is a lie that my mind was telling me, because all food is processed and used by our bodies. Our bodies are well-oiled machines that are a whole lot smarter than the logic our disordered minds try to use to define their functioning. These days even when the panic sets in, I try my best to push past. I know to give into those panicked thoughts would strengthen muscles I don't want anything to do with. I want to be toned by authenticity, normalcy, and freedom. I want peace. All I have ever wanted was some peace. In simpler terms, that meant I needed to get the fucking pizza.

Pizza and real soda, because to get diet soda would be an eating disorder win and I am not in the business of losing. I am competitive by nature. I want to win. I want to beat this disease that, for so many years, has taken over my mind. So, real soda is a must, and not just any real soda, but Root Beer.

This is a childhood favorite that I never allowed myself to have. Now, I have it when I want.

Don't get me wrong—these decisions to get what I want are hard as hell. I have to aim, fire, and shoot at the eating disorder multiple times throughout the day. The difference now is that the eating disorder doesn't have a chance—I am pulverizing it, devouring its very existence. The eating disorder is dying with each passing day, because I have been in enough therapy and I know too much about recovery to *not* fall into recovery. I can't unlearn all the skills and coping mechanisms that I have been taught. I have, in a way, been brainwashed into recovery. I have no choice, but a choice toward freedom. For this very fact, I will be eternally grateful to all of the therapists, dieticians, and fellow patients that have helped brainwash me along the way. With the help of a mini army, I have been given the gift of freedom.

08/17/18

The rain starts lightly, like the tapping of my fingers on the keyboard pitter pattering across the roof, the windows, the lamp posts, the streets. It coats the asphalt in a sheer sheet of glass, making it delicate, slippery, and misleading. The night crept up on me. The daylight was swallowed in sleep, tears, and pages of others' stories. I don't understand the stirring, twisting, gnawing pain in my gut that keeps me prisoner to my bed. It hurts worse than it has in months. This year was nearly free of this sickness, this knot in my gut, and yet here it is back with a vengeance.

I still have bad days.

"You're depressed. PTSD can manifest in this way sometimes. It is just flaring up right now. Be patient with yourself," professionals tell me through concerned stares and scribbling pencils.

"I'm broken," I explain.

There is a leak in my gut and insecurities, shame, rejection — they are all pouring in. I am slowly drowning in my own body. The leak, this crack, the hole in my gut — it's real, it's real, it's so damn real I can hardly breathe because my lungs are filling with the liquid of my tears, and my heart is weighed down by a thousand bricks of all the things that should have been said. *Do I even matter?* The demons creep back in, spewing their lies into my mind. Life starts to shrivel and the world becomes a pin hole that I no longer fit in. *I want to disappear*, I whisper under my breath as I fade into another dream. I want to be far away from all this pain, all this suffering, this sickness that will not go away.

"When did you start feeling this way again?"

Of course, the therapist would ask me. If she didn't, what was her degree for in the first place? This is a business arrangement, a chair worth thousands of dollars to help make me *better*. The cushion is sewn in my dollar bills pulled from my throat of hard work and perseverance.

"Just this week," I explained.

I can't remember because when the demons come, the days blur together. Colors melt and it all looks gray. Voices are muffled by the watery tears flooding my lungs all the way to my ear canal.

"What have you been doing to manage all this pain?" The therapist is relentless.

I roll my eyes, *"living."*

I live, I live, and I live. I want to shout. Living is getting up, eating, bathing, going to work on time, paying bills, and getting gas. I text people back. I hang out with friends. I do what is required because what the fuck am I supposed to do? Living is all that I know, and at the end of the day, I am a creature and creatures know how to survive. *I am in recovery*, I remind myself. Sometimes the feelings are too much, and all you have to do is survive. The feelings will pass. I've been here before. I know they will pass.

Flash forward to Monday morning—waking up early, drinking coffee, eating breakfast, listening to music, and writing. I am smiling as the sun rises. I am looking up the next country I will travel to.

It's night and day, yin and yang, dark and light. I have many persons, many demons, and many angels all within me. One day might be a rain shower of bullet casings, and the next a sunrise of unicorns. I'm not broken. I'm just crazy, and actually, I am okay with that because we all have crazy in us.

08/21/18

an ode to beauty culture

you take three steps forward
before jumping headfirst into a pit of cement
that you read in an ad was supposed to be a shower of
lilies
rainbows
and unicorns
you drive to the ER
with a mosaic of red between your eyes
you take a picture

you post a comment on the ad
and become the perfect pinnacle of sacrifice
beauty is pain
no pain no gain
what are you gaining
the ER nurse doesn't understand that
you were just showered in
lilies
rainbows
and unicorns
you jumped into a pile of cement
you show the nurse the picture
they get it now
everyone gets it
after all
only an idiot would jump into a pile of cement

08/27/18

Classical music in the early mornings is not a foreign concept. It feels repetitive—meditative. It puts me in a trance able to ease racing thoughts and any bodily discomfort. Mornings are a time of reflection—to sit and think, think, and think some more. Mornings are sacred. Mornings consist of mediation, reading, writing, and quietly staring off into the distance, allowing creativity to scream loud with exciting thoughts into these commonly absent ears.

I paint a lot. I draw a lot. I write a lot. I read a lot. Does that make me an artist? *Everyone is an artist,* is my response every time someone calls me one. I say this because I want so badly to be an artist that I am afraid of being one. Does that make sense? It is staring at the gold medal at the Olympics, afraid to take it out of the announcer's hand because once it touches your fingers, it is all real. Everything you worked for is real.

I had a dream last night that I was in the Olympics. I was an aerialist. They don't have that sport in the Olympics, but behind my closed eyelids, the competition was very real. I was the best, so naturally everyone hated me. I was ostracized from the team and forced to train on my own. Despite all odds, I won…? I actually woke up just before the results were in. I finished the dream for myself. I got the gold, and all my hard work paid off. I took the medal. I touched the gold. I allowed that dream to be achievable.

I've always been drawn toward seemingly impossible goals. When someone says *I wish I could just do* _____, I automatically want to do that thing. I want to prove to them and to myself that whatever they have deemed unachievable in their mind is actually within arm's reach. *Go do it! Go do it!* I always want to scream in people's faces, but that would be rude and uncalled for, and so I bite my tongue and let them vent about all the things that want to do in life but never will.

I don't want to have any regrets. I want to do whatever is on my bucket list. I want to be open to changes in my goals, to growth along the way. I never want to lose my determined spirit. I want, I want, I want… damn I want a lot of things.

Meditation helps me let go of all these racing ideas and thoughts. My therapist tells me that I need to be more present. I'm motivated, she says, which is good, but sometimes it's okay to *just be*. Yesterday, I tried to *just be*. I didn't know what to do, so I sat on my bed and listened to classical music and read. I don't think I give myself enough credit for how present I can be, each morning is filled with meditative and present rituals.

I like to write unconsciously, spilling all the thoughts onto paper as if to help sort them out. But, sometimes they don't need sorting. Sometimes they are fine just the way they are.

08/28/18

The fan buzzes to my left like a powerful and entrancing dragonfly. I used to be mesmerized by dragonflies, and in some ways, I still am. Three summers ago I went back to treatment. I had to stay in these supportive living apartments for people with eating disorders and mood problems. On my first night, I walked into my assigned apartment to find all the lights turned off, heavy metal blaring, and two shadowy figures on the couch. No one said hello. I put my bags down and left. I didn't feel welcome there.

The apartment was downtown Chicago, right next to Millennium Park. So I took the elevator down the twenty-seven or thirty-seven floors—I can't quite remember—and headed straight for the outdoor stadium. It was humid and hot—mid-August in Chicago, so it is to be expected—and I wore a long sleeved shirt and pants, because god forbid someone see my fat thighs and thumpy arms. They tell me to gain weight. I tell them to screw off. But none of that mattered as I sat there, alone, scared, and lost. Unable to comprehend how I got to this place again. I leaned back to lie down in the lawn and there I saw them. Hundreds upon hundreds of dragonflies. Buzzing, flying, dancing, mesmerizing me.

No one believed me. They tell me I must have imagined it. Why would there be a swarm of dragonflies randomly in Millennium Park, which no one else witnessed? I didn't care what they said. I didn't care what they thought. Whether imagined or real, the dragonflies were there. They danced for me, performing a composition I needed in that moment of fear and loneliness. They were there in my moment of questioning, all these weird little dancing bugs, keeping me company and making me feel a little less alone.

Maybe it is sad to think that bugs were my only source of company, or maybe it is sad for someone looking into my life, my story, because they don't understand the experiences that lead up to that moment. Being alone and able to have a moment to sit and reflect on my emotions, to witness the dragonflies, it felt like a miracle to me. Everything since moving to the city felt like a miracle to me.

It is amazing how dark times can be, and how light at the same time. It's the yin and yang, the good and the bad, the angels and the demons. I have a lot of both, I have decided. My demons are simply louder, while the angels are respectful and pleasant. They scream and scream and scream about my dirty little used up good for nothing body. I have learned to sit and wait it out, to let them throw their fit. Scream and yell and make me feel like shit, that's how they find pleasure. The demons are just like them – the people who took my personhood, who stole from me, who robbed me of understanding what respect is, what love is, what kindness is.

Hit. Slam. Blood. Pain. Inside of me. Outside of me. All over me. Yelling. Tears. *"Don't cry, you little bitch."* I don't cry ever again. I remember. I see the images every time the demons scream their bloody heads off. I see them, and hear them, and live them, but I don't believe them. That just can't be me—if that were me, how am I still me? How am I still walking around—still living, breathing, laughing, crying, hoping, and praying? How am I still human when so much of my spirit was sucked straight out of me?

It all comes back to the dragonflies, and how I see miracles every day. I look in the mirror and see a miracle. I let Erik kiss me and I witness a million miracles. I am blessed by hundreds of dancing dragonflies that no one else sees. I pet a shark underwater and feel as if I have just uncovered the truth about the entire order of the universe. I run through forests and the trees sing to me. I look up at the sky and tears fall down my cheeks, because I know. I know more than

anyone else there is something up there orchestrating a shit
ton of miracles for us to encounter every day—but if you
aren't looking you're going to miss them. You see, I've been
through enough hell to notice when something is not from
the pits of fire and despair. All I have known is burning
sensations and tears of Clorox, so when I feel a breeze of
goodness or taste words of kindness, I see these things, I feel
these things, I understand these things on a different level.
These touches of light—the new song on the radio, the text
from a friend, the hug from a stranger, the parking spot in
front of the store—these are miracles. Some of us are just too
blind to see.

08/31/18

Staring can become a safe place. Therapists ask you to create one when you first walk into treatment, a place that you can go in your mind when you're feeling overwhelmed. I don't have a place. I have a blank, numbed out, stare down with the wall. Apparently it's called dissociation, and it's a symptom of Post-Traumatic Stress Disorder. But anyone who knows what it's like to question whether you will survive a moment, knows how safe staring can become.

At the height of it all, I could stare at the ceiling and completely escape the world. I would become separate from myself, a floating miracle made up of particles, too numerous to catch and too quick to see. After a certain point, I wouldn't remember what happened, that's how well versed I became in the art of staring. Memories were completely gone, or rather unwritten. They were stamped into my brain as moments of disconnection, of floating around the ceiling fans of unknown spaces at unknown times. Memories are now blacked out with a Sharpie, blacklisted from my mind. It's the body that brings me back. The body that remembers everything. That's how I know things happen. My body is the key.

My body and I were enemies for many years. It tugged and whined and pleaded with me to acknowledge the pain it was going through. Instead, I did the opposite. I starved it, cut it, abused it for years until its poor weak little frame almost gave up. It was only then that I realized if the body gave up, then the mind was gone as well. And my mind, well, it seemed like a hero after all the years of hell. So I attempted to sew the broken shattered pieces back together. Nutrition, stitches, heart monitors, and pills became a recipe toward health, toward recovery. I never understood why professionals wanted to help a little shit like me. Why they were nice, why they asked to talk, gave me skills, sat with me during fits of tears and hopelessness—I didn't understand their kindness. It was an unfamiliar concept to me after telling myself I was undeserving for so long.

Right now, I miss the disconnection between my mind and body. I miss the days when I didn't feel my gut or pain, when I was totally numb to the physical world around me. I get sad, really sad. Not the kind of sad where you cry, or stay in bed, or don't reach out to anyone. This is the kind of sad where you don't know if you'll survive another moment in this god forsaken life, where you're desperately searching for answers to the question of *why me?* Why do I have to go through this? Why do I have to be so lonely? Why do I have to endure so much pain?

My biggest fear in life is loneliness, and yet that is what I feel every day. Maybe my biggest fear is that I will never *not* feel lonely, that I will always have this pain deep in my heart that whispers that I will never actually be okay. That being okay only existed as an illusion of makeup, diets, weight loss, plastic surgeons, and a size X pair of jeans. Okay was when I ate everything and then emptied it out in a toilet bowl of blood and food particles. It was the pain of cutting, the harshness of my words. Okay was the opposite of okay, meaning I never understood what safety truly meant in the first place.

So I sit here, with the incense burning and the pittering of the keyboard mixed with soft jazz keeping me comfort because I am, once again, terribly lonely. The kind of lonely that makes me wonder if I can survive another moment. But I know I have been here before. I was here yesterday and the day before, and I survived. I survive through words, through art, through music, and other people's stories. I survive for the child within me and the future children that I will raise because that will, for damn sure, be given the chance to create a safe scene, know what kindness is, and understand that they will always be okay.

09/05/18

Recovery is not linear.
Recovery is not linear.
Recovery is not linear.
Recovery…..is…..not…..

I have heard it a thousand times. In fact, I have heard it so much, that the words have started to disintegrate the minute they fall out of a professional's mouth. I'm not asking for linear. I just want relief. I want a surgeon to go into my brain and remove the parasite that has made its home between my sanity and freedom.

Don't misunderstand me. I am in recovery. I am the farthest I have ever been in recovery. Months are passing and I am slowly becoming more and more of myself, but I have these nights. These god-forsaken nights where everything folds in on itself and I am left curled into a little ball of confusion and desperation. And when I feel small, conflicted, and stressed, I want to lose weight. I dream about it, I fantasize about numbers, I pinch at my skin, and I revel at the release removing this layer of cellulite would bring me. It's my default. Same as a drug addict craving a hit. I crave emptiness, numbness. I am addicted to food. I know that. I am constantly reminded of this fact.

My day was perfect. The morning was great—peaceful. I went to a bookstore and spent way too much money on books that excited every cell in my body. Books are my high. They have always been there for me. The stories can bring me far, far away from reality. I could read for weeks, never speaking to anyone, and be the happiest girl in the world. Of course, that would be unhealthy—and a little weird by societal standards—so instead, I limit myself to hours at a time with incense and jazz music playing in the background. Therapists always tell you that you need a safe place. I've recently decided, this is mine.

Anyways, the morning was great. Had some avocado toast, listened to Trevor Hall's new album, and drank a latte that was poured by the gods. Then I walked into therapy, and everything started to shift. The air in the office was thick. I felt suffocated, uneasy. I wanted to turn around and run away, but I always feel this way when I walk into therapy. It is in this tiny little office on the third floor that I am confronted with all the issues I ignore throughout the week. I am asked how I am, what I need to talk about, and I shrug. It is the usual routine. I never know. I always feel fine, like there's nothing to be discussed. I am eating, and apparently that translates as nothing is wrong in my life.

Therapy leaves me walking like a maniac down the sidewalk. I am checking my email, Instagram, texting people back. I can't do just one thing. I need my mind to race with many thoughts and tasks in order to keep this panicked energy at bay. *I am manic. I am manic.* I am sure that I am manic right now, but I just had a session…it could be anxiety. It could be mania. I could be dying of some brain tumor that is pressing on the sane part of my mind and turning me crazy. The possibilities are endless, but my doctor just increased my meds, so I rule out mania. I have no other symptoms of a brain tumor, and I fall back on – I am panicking.

I turn on my car. The gas light is on, and I can't pay for gas. The cost is so high right now, but I Google gas stations and pick the one with the lowest price. I start driving. Traffic is awful, my hands are shaking, but I make it to the gas station only to realize it is the Costco one, and the line is crazy long.

I am not even sure that I can get gas here, because I am not a member of the Costco tribe, so I go to the next gas station. There's another line. I wait and wait and wait. It starts pouring, and traffic is getting worse. I need to get to work by 5:00 p.m. I will never make it by 5:00. I call my boss. She doesn't answer, so I call the house. My co-counselor picks up, and I tell her to ask someone to help her make dinner. She says no one else is there. I swear, and I tell her I am sorry. I'll be there as soon as possible. I beat myself up about being an idiot for spending so much at the bookstore. I put the gas on my credit card—at least I'll get rewards points for traveling. I get on the highway and suddenly, everyone has forgotten how to drive because of the rain. I try to sing to music. I am still panicking. Nothing is helping. I roll into work a half hour late. I frantically start preparing dinner, and things seem okay for a moment. I start to get in a grove and I talk to the patients. They make me feel at home. They make me feel welcome. They make me feel like I have a purpose. Work is good. It keeps me busy, but then as the shift comes to a close, I start to spiral. The panic I shoved down the moment I walked into work resurfaces, and all I can think about is the eating disorder. I start dreaming about it, planning my relapse, how to get to the grocery store, how to lose weight, how to binge, how to get a scale, on and on and on. My mind is relentless. I can't turn it off. I start pinching the dimples on my thighs and panicking about how large I have gotten. Everything feels bleak and hopeless. I drive home. I listen to Julien Baker's "Turn Out the Lights" and everything changes…

Do you ever have those moments when the perfect song comes on at the perfect time? Baker's song is bleak, but it spoke to me, and I was reminded of tomorrow. That even these hard moments in recovery, even the worst days are only twenty-four hours long. Ride the wave. Come on

Morgan, ride the wave. Don't do something you are going to regret in the morning. I drive straight home and immediately get into bed. I close my eyes and sigh. I made it. The demons didn't catch me. I made it another day. I made it through another battle, and I fall asleep—exhausted from the war I have been fighting for years and years and years.

09/09/18

There's a certain euphoria that accompanies watching the water. The bend, curves, and movement of the droplets, each have their own personality. It's mesmerizing to imagine all these little drops of water dancing together to make up such an amazing example of the order of everything. I have been, and always will be, enchanted by the water. We have a love for one another that is unexplainable, but the relationship doesn't exist among words because the connection does not make sense in this reality. It is a spiritual bond. I feel it in the smile on my face, the kiss of the cool water on my skin, and the beauty of the dancing waves.

The waves are huge tonight. The water is angry. It crashes and screams against the concrete barrier which I am sitting on while the wind howls and the sky is gray, giving the water a greenish hue. The crashes echo into the air, creating a melody so sweet and powerful, that I can't help but laugh along. The water dots my cheeks and I giggle with each touch. Suddenly, I am a small child experiencing everything for the first time. There is a magic in these moments, and I am completely at peace.

My mood shifts as quickly as the water's waves. Just minutes before as I was driving toward the water, I felt on the verge of tears. There was a deep rooted darkness spreading rapidly in my gut, up toward my throat, leaving me silent and uncomfortable. Now here, everything feels like complete bliss. I am light and clear, and the darkness has shrunk once more. My voice returns in the form of laughter and joy, and I no longer feel connected to the dark figure that rode here along with me.

These mood swings have been happening frequently over the last couple of weeks. I am riding them out, which is a new concept for me. Before, I would jump headfirst into the darkness, believing its lies as I slowly drown into self-hatred. But that cycle didn't work, it never worked, it never will work. So, I am trying something different. It's called waiting. And waiting and waiting and waiting, with the hope that something will change. Of course, I do other things—coping skills, as the professionals would say. Meditation, yoga, art, music, and lots and lots of reading. These skills are supposed to turn things around, lighten my moods, make me feel less dark and heavy. Maybe they do help, but the change is so slight that I don't notice. I suppose I believe in change, because I keep doing these skills and waiting for things to turn around.

But nothing the professionals have taught me compares to the gentle hug I receive from the water. I find myself commonly singing around my apartment the *Moana* soundtrack, *"I've been staring at the edge of the water..."* and so on. My roommates and boyfriend laugh at it, but they know. They know that I am, in fact, just like Moana. I feel this connection with the ocean, deeper than any connection on land. It gives me joy by simply being along its shore. I am a child in love for the first time. It calls to me, sings to me, talks to me—and suddenly, I am the hippy grandmother from Moana dancing on the beach while the manta rays encircle me.

My name means Lady of the Sea. Is it the ultimate irony? Have I unconsciously adopted the love for the ocean because I knew the meaning of my name from a young age? Or was this name meant to be, specifically chosen for me from some spiritual realm unknown, at the time, by my parents? We all can believe our own answers to these questions. I don't dwell on them. I just love that even my name points me towards the water. What a gift, what a friend, what a complete punch in the face to the loneliness that my demons spill upon me.

I sit and watch. I close my eyes and allow the midst of the waves to kiss my cheeks. I say a prayer. I meditate. I film the crashing of the water against the concrete and then I leave. I leave knowing that I will be back tomorrow and the next day and every day after that. I leave knowing if I continue to nurture this love, no darkness will ever overcome me again.

09/11/18

It's 8:00 p.m., but it feels like 2:00 a.m. I spent all of last night tapping my foot against the wall and counting the shadowy lines through the window panes. I'm in Florida, somewhere in the woods, in a cabin by an underground cave that I'll be scuba diving in tomorrow. I love it. I love the taste of adventure fresh on the tip of my tongue, and the promise of the water that the next sunrise is going to bring—but I also struggle, even on vacations, even on adventures.

I forgot all of my medication in Chicago. I realized it at 11:00 p.m. last night, and my heart sank. Of all things, of all the damn things I could have forgotten, it had to be the medicine—the one thing that isn't easily accessible to me when I am driving around the southern forests looking for random caves to jump in to. I had to make frantic calls and find a CVS the next morning. I felt nauseous from the lack of medication last night, and my heart was racing because I didn't take the pill that keeps the arrhythmia at bay.

I have a chill personality, but a racing mind. I have so many ideas and thoughts and plans and dreams that jump behind my eyelids with each passing moment. The tree on my left inspired a short story playing out behind my right eyelid while the song in my ear helps choreograph a modern dance piece behind my other eye. Call it the syndrome of a creative. Call it the artist's madness. Call it whatever you want, but there are moments where I lose it. Not externally — externally I have never been calmer – but internally I am a bucket of boiling lava that is raging a war against my intestines and throat.

I started making a list of all the things I needed to accomplish when I got home. At what point did my racing thoughts turn from creativity to anxiety? I couldn't tell you—perhaps somewhere between arguing with the pharmacist and incessantly calling my psychiatrist, hoping that she would call back. But, there was a switch and suddenly the adventures of my friend and I in the forest, scuba diving, and camping in tree houses became an obsessive search of the vaccines I never got and what diseases I am now going to die from. I don't know why, of all things to worry about, vaccines popped into my head. Maybe because I had been dealing with doctors to try to figure out my medication? Who knows why the mind does what it does? But either way, I Googled Walgreens clinics next to me and tried to make an appointment. I mean, might as well go in tomorrow so that I don't worry for my entire trip, right? Plus, if I wait another day before being vaccinated, I could be infected tomorrow and I'd never forgive myself.

The mind is a crazy machine. It needs to be carefully watched and attuned, or else it may run rampant and convince you that you should spend your time in rural Florida searching for a Walgreens clinic instead of diving the underwater cave a hundred yards from your cabin.

Flash forward to passing out around 8:45 p.m., and waking up to the 90 degree heat of the morning after a night's rest and the magic of sleep. Sleep has a remarkable ability to reset the mind and challenge my irrational thoughts, worries, and obsessions. I decided the mix of sleep deprivation and forgetting my medication resulted in the panic. I'm sure anyone reading this would have been able to figure that one out, but when you're trapped in that moment, everything feels so real, so heavy, so extreme.

Yesterday was a day heightened by anxiety. Today was a day enlightened by adventure.

Diving into that cave...

The thrill of swimming through those small crevices...

The beauty of the pictures...

The moments cherished...

09/16/18

When I was in Costa Rica in February, everyone gathered on
the beach with drums and ribbons to dance, howl, and sing
as the sun set. There was a loud roar from the entire crowd
when the sun made its final descent along the horizon.
When the party slowly faded and the sky turned from pink
to purple, we all packed up and filed like little ants back into
our tents in the forest before it got too dark to see anything.

When I was in Thailand in June, we sat on the beach singing
mantras and strumming guitars while lying on our backs in
a circle. We sang louder and howled as the sky turned pink
and the sun dipped away for the night. We stayed on the
beach until twilight and the mosquitoes became unbearable.
Then we went back to our bungalows, made curry, and
danced with our host family's young daughter.

Today, I was sitting on a deck in Key Largo watching the
sunset over the ocean's horizon while listening to Tash
Sultana and laughing with my best friends. We smiled and
argued over whose picture captured the sky's beauty the
best—even though the pictures were nearly the same. Then
we sat in rocking chairs and talked nonsense before coming
inside to prepare for tomorrow's day full of adventures.

Nighttime tends to be the most difficult for me. It is the time
when urges are heightened and nightmares come to life
behind my closed eyelids. It is where I lie in the dark, afraid
of the hurt child inside me. It is when my stomach is bloated
from a day's food and I take another sleep aid to try to calm
my racing mind—which has suddenly convinced me that I
am nothing but cellulite. The dark brings the demons out in
me. The shadows of the night and the demons from my past

are best friends. They speak to one another underneath the black sky like old lovers—embracing and precious.

Some nights are full of tender moments, moments that make my soul smile and my heart race—like last night when my friend and I stayed at this man's house in Coco beach. It was just a room that he rented out for $20 dollars a person. This man, Charles, was older and single, and he said he gets lonely and likes meeting interesting people. There was another guy staying in the back room. We all chatted, ate rice and beans, watched *Avatar*, and swam in the pool. The night was peaceful. It was free of the voices in my head, but I woke up the next day to my friend telling me I kept hitting and pushing her away in my sleep. I shrugged it off, but there was a sinking in my stomach. Even on nights where I believe the peace I always pray for has finally overtaken the demons, I am reminded of those memories in my head.

"Nightmares...I have nightmares sometimes," I explained. "I'm sorry."

Suddenly I am embarrassed and hurry to finish Charles's dishes. I don't want people to know I still struggle. I don't want people to know the truth behind my recovery journey.

Two nights ago I was in the forest, dancing to Ben Howard at midnight in this room called the Glass Castle. As the music continued, the harder I danced. There was passion pouring out of my fingers, anger expelling from my feet. I felt powerful—so damn powerful. Then, the music stopped. I noticed the sweat covering my legs and stomach. I noticed the dark. I laid down. I closed my eyes and listened as the next song began. I sang along, humming mainly because I didn't know the words. A peace rushed over me. A sensation of gratitude and longing. Longing for time to bend and swallow me into this memory. Everything just felt right, because while completely encapsulated by the music and night, everything made sense.

Recovery, like everyone always says, is not linear. There are ups and downs, twists and turns. Sometimes you go left when the map wanted you to take a right, but you get rerouted and everything turns out in the end—if only you keep moving. But, recovery is so much more than that.

Recovery is simply *life*.

The sunsets, the nightmares at Charles's, the dancing in the forest—these were all moments that reminded me of what it means to be human. I have these divine realizations of the beauty of each passing day, the celebration with communities about the coming night and the promise of the next sunrise. I have dark moments, like nightmares, that keep me grounded. They remind me where I come from. They remind me of my strength, my resilience, my continued hope. Then there is the dancing and the freedom of my movements—the sweat, the heavy breathing, the music, the ground beneath my body, and the intensely black forest sky above my head. These are the moments of understanding. These are the moments when this crazy recovery journey I have been on, for a second, appears in my mind as a cohesive narrative.

09/24/18

Sounds of a rushing stream trickle out of my phone, trying to trick my brain into thinking I'm not actually in my bedroom on the third floor of an apartment complex in downtown Chicago. My roommate isn't vacuuming, and my downstairs neighbors aren't blasting shitty pop music. It's the illusion of calm—the roaring fan blowing cold air, the phone singing of rushing water, the candles flickering, offering up the scent of vanilla and toasted coconut. I trick my mind into believing I'm somewhere in the forest, burning incense and sleeping under the stars. But, in turn, my mind tricks me into believing I am fat, unwanted, and all alone. It's a trade-off, an unwritten contract, an agreement made some time ago that neither of us can seem to let go of. It's a habit at this point, one that I am slowly trying to break.

It's like trying to stop biting your nails. At first, you don't even realize you're doing it, until your thumb is between your teeth and the top part of the nail is ripped off. Awareness is the first step—I tell this to the girls I work with all the time. We don't want to hear that because it suggests that the process standing in front of us is more intense than we expected. But, awareness *is* the first step. It's also my fall back point. I find myself daydreaming about losing weight so I light the candles. I start heading toward the scale at the gym so I listen to the stream. I lie in bed reminiscing on depressed thoughts so I turn on the fan and allow myself to fall asleep in order to reset.

I trick my mind to keep my mind from tricking me. I used to believe it was a trade-off, a balanced relationship, one that would always leave me on the same level as my mental illnesses. I thought recovery was just about managing

symptoms and thoughts and behaviors. Take my meds, eat
my food, go to therapy—wash, rinse, and repeat. I started to
lose track of the days, but somewhere through the last
couple of months, I have risen above the tricks of my mind.
I have found ways around them. Awareness became
planning and planning lead to fighting back. The sounds of
the stream, the candles, the fan, my art, my books, my
snacks, the pool, the medication in my cabinet—these aren't
tricks, anymore. These things are my safety net. They make
me feel safe when my mind is a battleground. I have found
weapons to quiet the cannons and gunshots. I know the
secret now. Sometimes I just forget I have the tools.

* * *

09/24/18

It's late and maybe it's just this moment, but all my anxieties
have aligned and are screaming at me to shrink, to whither,
to become small and useless just like I feel. I want to die,
sometimes. It's still there in moments like this. I think of the
sweet release that the endless darkness would bring. No
more anxiety or pain or worry, no more trauma or eating
disorder or or or....no more Erik, no more yoga, no more art,
no more sister or brother or cousins, no more music, car
rides, coffee…maybe it isn't dying, but losing weight that I
want. I want my love handles gone, and the dimples on my
thighs and the fullness of my cheeks to disintegrate. I want
to be thin again. I want to be sick and small and hurting
because that's how I feel. Inside reflecting the outside—it's
all that currently makes sense.

I work with very sick girls. I see myself in the hollow eyes
and refusal to eat. I see myself in the pain and suddenly I'm

sucked in, swallowed in the despair and longing to become one of them again. I want what they have—the call for help, the representation of pain, a means of hurting themselves. It's insanity, doing the same thing over and over and believing in different results. The eating disorder does nothing for me, and yet somehow I long for it to kiss me one more time. To hold me, caress me, feed me the lies of my worthlessness until I'm numb enough to stop caring. I want a release. All I've ever wanted was a release.

I want to rip off the winter coat I am forced to wear year round. I want a release from the suffocating feeling that is my own skin. I want to carve out my fat and muscles and tissues until there's only bone, just a walking dead little skeleton, like the ones that hide in my closet.

I'm tired and panicky. My heart is starting to race like it used to last year—beat beat beat beat, hot, sweaty, and stars whenever I stand. It's only been one hour, and I've written this in incriminates, because I periodically have to stop and ground myself.

I am supposed to be doing shift notes, but I'm too busy flirting with my own disorder to focus on my job. *I miss you,* it says, and I say it back because suddenly I feel young and in love, and stricken by the desire to be hated once more. It's messed up, I know. I tell the girls it is okay to eat the brownie because all foods fit, and then I pinch and measure my arm with my fingers to make sure the stupid brownie didn't make me blow up like a balloon.

Some days, I'm okay. Some days, I don't even think about this messed up shit. I have to remind myself of this fact because it is the only thing tethering me to the world. I feel like I'm constantly floating along somewhere in the atmosphere disconnected from everyone and everything, but there's this little tiny string that ties me down, keeps me from floating into space forever. I always wonder what that string is. Hope, perhaps? My Higher Power? Purpose? All of that feels superficial and naive in moments like this.

I pinch my thigh dimples and count the taps of my thumbs until I get to X.

X pounds—that's how much I want to lose.

But maybe I don't really want to lose anything. Maybe I am just so terrified of keeping everything, that emptiness is all I crave? I crave the despair and hollowness because it is all I know. Familiarity is the comforter I curl into at night, snuggling the darkness's nightmares. I throw punches at Erik and shake throughout these black hours. He tells me in the morning that "I just squeeze you tighter in those moments". I want to scream, *"Why are you so nice to me,"* because it is truly hard to conceptualize someone as caring as him.

I swallow another pill and pray that this time, it will chisel the happiness it promises into my bones. The funny thing is I am happy, the happiest I have ever been, but sometimes I get caught in this painful awareness of the claws on my back. They scratch and tear, but I have built up callouses over the years so I don't really feel them anymore. I just catch a glimpse every once in a while and get derailed, but then I smell morning coffee, or jump into the water, and the claws aren't so powerful anymore.

I have good things.
I have good things.
The claws don't matter anymore.

09/25/18

My legs are scratching me. I haven't had time to shave.
Shaving irritates my chlorinated skin and makes me break
out in rashes. I have tried every remedy, so I don't need any
more suggestions of tricks to fight razor burn. It's the pool.
The chemicals in it dry out my skin and make me itch. I get
it. I submerge them in chlorine almost every day now, but I
have to. It is an obsession, a deep love affair with the water.
I can't explain it, but when my mind is too much, jumping
into that cold pool suddenly makes everything okay again.
I am suspended in this substance that leaves me weightless.
The room turns silent. All I can hear is my breathing, and
there's finally a moment of pause. For those laps in the pool
– that rhythmic dance between my arms and legs as I repeat
freestyle over and over again – I will trade for razor burned,
scratchy legs.

I've been listening to Julien Baker for the last two days which
isn't a good sign. She's my fall back when I need to know
someone else has experienced rock bottom. My rock
bottom's year anniversary is coming up in a few weeks —
October 19th. My therapist asked me how I felt about it.

"You mean, how do I feel about surviving my overdose?" I
deadpanned. "I try not to think about last year."

And then the conversation switches. My therapist tries to
pull it back, but I push harder. I am the one paying for these
sessions, so I guess she decides to give up and go along with
my tangent about angels and God and all this other spiritual
shit. I don't like the darkness. I don't want to look at it, don't
want to feel it, and I certainly don't want to remember it.
Last October was the worst month of my life – I have been
through some real shit, so that is saying something. The

ambulance, the ER, the hospital, it all mixed together to become the most humiliating, shameful, and scarring experience of my life. I was an animal in there. An animal whose humanity was stripped away and all that mattered was being able to keep me locked up so I didn't infect the rest of the world.

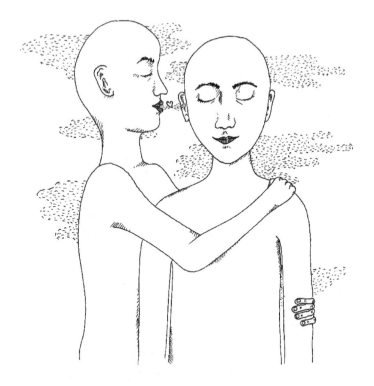

09/28/18

I rested my head down on my stuffed dog that I have clung to for the last four years. Maple has been with me through some of the worst. Maple never, ever made me feel unsafe.

But really this wasn't about Maple at all. It wasn't about stuffed dogs or my bed or this moment. It was about all the moments leading up to this one. I love him. I love Erik more than I knew I could love. Maple is there and always will be, but Erik is my new safe point. He holds me and whispers his love into my ear. He is strong and steady. He adores me and I adore him.

10/01/18

Somewhere between the time it took for Microsoft to open and my hands to hit the keyboard, I broke. As the icon kept bouncing up and down, I held my breath, waiting and waiting and waiting for the empty page to appear on the screen so that I could purge everything boiling up inside of me, so that I could keep from running to the toilet conveniently located next to my bedroom and tear the cake from my gut through newly chiseled knives I wore as fingertips, so that I could appease the demons inside my brain as if the click clack of my fingernails on the keys could do anything close to that.

Somewhere in that empty space of waiting, a shower of everything dark and everything heavy and everything so hard and hurtful flooded my mind in one large typhoon, and suddenly the wrinkles of cellulite on my legs caused me more pain than the memories flashing behind my eyelids. Suddenly, my body was not my own, and the thunder outside my window wasn't mother earth's orchestra, but rather gunshots targeted at the space between my legs. I felt attacked, attacked and betrayed from the very skin I was supposed to call my own. The freckles that once created a map to the years spent living inside these bones, these tissues, these organs, these experiences became pressure points for a body slowly dying. I wanted to tear the layers apart—carve out the freckles, turn myself inside out, and leave the blood to wash away in the rain – because I didn't want this person anymore. Somewhere in the time between opening this blank document and beginning to write, my body turned on me and I once again fell victim to its cruelty.

Except my body isn't cruel. My body was never cruel. My body was beaten by words, shrunken, starved, and forced to swallow screams down its throat. My body was torn down through the violence of those arrogant enough to think they could hold a fortress such as mine. My body exploded in their face, my tears melted their skin. I left a scar in the space where their heart once had been and, for that, they will forever remember me. Just as I will forever remember the violation that they spent millions to purchase, to win me as a prize as if a human—a young child was a prize to be won and not a treasure to be protected.

The moment when I broke, I shattered. Parts of myself— parts of my story, parts of my demons and angels, saints and refugees—all scatter across my room, but it was late and I didn't have the willpower to patch myself back together. So I closed my eyes and waited for the pieces that were truly mine—the soft breasts, the round hips, the beating heart full of passion and grace, the red hair fiery and strong, the freckled map, the rosy cheeks, the humility, the honor—to grow legs and collect themselves across my hurting body. They became a mosaic armor of protection and remembrance of what I truly had fought to become.

10/02/18

There are nights when my mind slithers through my eyes, swims across the room, and sits in the corner staring smugly back at me. And since my mind is the powerhouse for this accumulation of randomness I call thoughts, it has the authority to convince me that nothing is real and everything is a dream. Why else would my mind be able to escape my body and look at me from across the room? I am lying in my bed while simultaneously watching myself lie in my bed while simultaneously panicking about lying in my bed. I'm split in three parts: the body that is physically attached to the blankets and mattress, the mind that is escaping reality and floating somewhere yards away, and my memories which are convincing me that I am not safe, that I need to run away before the truth about my past is revealed and I end up reliving it.

Dissociation. That's what the therapists would call it.

Dissociation literally means the disconnection or separation of something from something else, or the state of being disconnected. So, in my case, my mind is separated from my body. I operate on two different playing fields—an emotional and a physical—and there's no saying which one ends up being *real* in the end.

10/05/18

By the time I was eleven, I had lived eleven lifetimes. Each year felt like another world. It just so happened that eleven became the apocalypse that no one warned me was coming.

Everything around me was dry and desolate. The slightest obstacle in my routine became a life threatening situation. Starve, school, dance, run, starve some more, and try to sleep. I became hostile to everyone around—icing out friends, teachers, anyone who started to come near. Come too close to me, and an alarm was triggered. I saw danger in everyone. All I wanted, all I wanted, all I wanted was to not want anything.

So at eleven, I stopped eating, because somehow I learned that starvation left me hollow enough to leave the world. If people tried to talk to me, all they would receive was an endless echo reverberating off my hollow frame. I was a shell. Here, but not actually here. All organs had run away to find solace in a body that was actually living. All I was left with were my bones, skin, and the fake smile I wore on my freckled face. No one seemed to even notice that my heart had run away, or that my lungs had abandoned me, or that my stomach ate itself. No one noticed, and therefore at eleven, I decided that no one actually cared.

I wore my hair in two Princess Leia buns every day to school. There were twenty-one bobby pins in each, which made forty-two in total. My principal had this game of trying to guess the number of pins it took to do my hair. He was always wrong and the number was always the same. I ate eight grapes at lunch because I Googled and found out each grape has five calories, so to have ten would be too much—ten would be fifty calories which is too close to a hundred, so I subtracted two and settled on forty. I worked out multiple times a day. I measured my waist in the morning and at night. If it was bigger at night, I hit myself ten times. I weighed myself three times each time I got on the scale and took the average of the numbers. I didn't trust the one scale so I walked to the store, bought another scale, and weighed myself three times on each, and took the average of all my calculations. I went to bed at 10:00 p.m. and woke up at 5:00 a.m. I never really slept so instead I counted the taps of my thumbs against my thighs. *One, two, three…*

Numbers kept me sane during a time when I was anything but. Here I was, this child, terrified, silent, and angry with no idea why she was this way. But the most unsettling part was that I had never felt more in control. As the year went on, the apocalypse continued, and I managed to stay afloat. I had a skill that no one else could take from me. I could lose weight. I could make my body do what I wanted it to. I could shrink away memories, starve out those images, numb the wincing, run off the sensations. I was powerful in this way.

A powerful little eleven-year-old anorexic.

But when I was eleven, there wasn't anyone around to tell me that powerful and anorexic couldn't coexist.

10/10/18

There's no telling how long it will be tonight before my eyelids actually close and my mind turns to madness. It's better this way, better for me to lie on my side, staring blankly at the wall, counting the taps of my thumbs against my thighs. It is better to feel nothing, to dissociate from the space around me, to become a particle floating around in space. Isn't that what we all are? Particles. These little dots of existence in a massive universe. There are things way up there that my brain couldn't even fathom, and yet it is sleep that scares me. I turn to my other side and hug my stuffed dog closer to my chest as I fall into my inner child — lonely, scared, and anticipating chaos to erupt at any moment.

He sang to me today. He held me and whispered I was safe and that he loved me. Then he sang. He sang to my inner child, calmed her, and I cried. He didn't ask what the flashback was about. He didn't ask me why I had them. He didn't ask me anything. He just held me and sang, *"Blackbird singing in the dead of night, take these broken wings and learn to fly...all my life you were only waiting for this moment to be free..."* I silently cried. My stomach contracted as I swallowed sobs. No one has ever loved me the way that he does.

Maybe love could be the antidote for all of this pain — maybe love could suck it away and drip peace down my parched throat. Faith is a special gift I keep locked deep inside. It was a present given to me at fourteen, and it has never left me since. Faith is believing in what you cannot see. Faith is jumping off the cliff, not knowing what will meet you at the bottom, but believing that it is better than the dark forest you traveled through to get there. Faith is falling and building yourself wings....or is that resiliency? I think faith and resiliency are the same. One cannot exist without the other. To be resilient you must have faith. Through having faith you become resilient. I don't know why, but I have these seeds inside of me, and they have always been right there, in the middle of my spirit. Whatever I wish to create for my life will happen. How? Through love. Love for life, love for myself, love for opportunities, but above all—unconditional love for those around me. When you send love out, it comes back. Love is a circle. It is never-ending. Those you love you have always loved. You just weren't aware of the love because the universe hadn't shown you that person yet. But they were there, and your spirit knew because of the longing in your gut. You knew your person was out there, you needed them, and then all the sudden you have them.

Now, I think I am talking about soulmates. Many people believe you have multiple soulmates in this lifetime. I think there is one. You have one person chiseled out by the universe as the perfect gift for you. You are each other's best friends. You make each other better humans. You laugh together. You cry together. You are each other's go-to person. Soulmates are a once-in-a-lifetime experience. Ask anyone. They always have that one person they can't seem to shake. Whether it worked out or not—that was their soulmate, but it takes a shit ton of faith to believe in such a powerful statement. Luckily, I have accumulated a lot of faith over the years. I have been an expert at conjuring it and holding it close to my heart. I have enough faith to write down that Erik is my soulmate, and I knew it within a month of dating him. He was the one I would spend the rest of my life with. What a big statement coming from a girl with a history like mine, one where trust felt impossible, and connection was dangerous. Take a breath and digest that for the night, and I'll just go back to staring at the wall and tapping my thumbs until I feel safe enough to fall asleep.

10/12/18

What does it mean when someone whispers *Jesus Christ* at your story? What does it mean when people look down and away, when they no longer text you, when they fly halfway across the country because your big fat mouth scared them away? What does it mean to share lies that bleed through your teeth, staining another's white shirt red? What does it mean when someone eats the blood like chocolate, and holds you as if you've suffered a great loss? What happens when your voice becomes a growl, your hands claws, and your freckles black numbers marking all the times that you fucked up?

I connected the black numbers dotting my body. They came together to make one large spider—a creepy, crawling, hairy spider. People ran. I wasn't a person anymore. I was a giant venomous insect. I was terrifying. *You're all lucky*, I wanted to scream. *You're all lucky because at least you can run away.*

I washed off my sins but the black wouldn't rinse, so I bleached my skin and dyed my hair red. And suddenly everything became fake and real and upside-down and crooked at the same time. *Is this your natural hair color?* People ask me all the time. I nod, but never mention I fought for this god damn hair through bleach and shame and horror and agony. This red hair is mine whether it's natural or not, because what is natural when you were born a victim in your own skin?

Who are you, if not yourself? Who do you become the moment yourself dies, but your body is still there—floating in space, walking on air? Every word spoken to me was muffled by the sound of waves. I couldn't quite make out the words. All I saw was concerned faces staring at my disconnected body. *Someone cut the cord.* I wanted to tell them. Cut the cord that fused my body and mind. Now I was just swimming, swimming in a sea of words and distorted landscapes. I wasn't there. I wasn't gone. Time stopped and dropped me inside its frozen little capsule. Time is cruel that way. It leaves you behind while marching on its merry way.

When you were a child, did you stare at the sun? Did you howl at the moon? Did you catch bugs and eat them? Chew on dirt? Stomp on pretzels and then pick up the broken pieces? Odd. People called me odd all the time. Odd and strange, peculiar, out of place. I didn't fit in my body and I didn't fit in the time given. I saw fairies and leprechauns, aliens and UFOs. I knew my guardian angel by name and whispered to demons in the dark. My head was not connected to my body, because my body was tied to the ground. I knew there was more. There always had to be more.

How did you make it through? A follow-up question from every professional.

I told myself that there was more than this darkness. I told myself stories about angels and demons and magical parts of the world. I watched videos about the galaxies and studied the smallest creatures. I went diving in the oceans and climbed to the tallest mountaintops, all to prove to my demons that there was more—there was so much more.

Even now when I lie in bed—when I am scared and small, clutching my stuffed animals like a child—I remind myself of the galaxies, of the seahorses, of the bioluminescence, of the clouds, the moon, the rivers, and valleys. I am small and scared, but there are things out there waiting to be explored.

10/16/18

I walk to blink my eyes and stare ahead without any knowledge of how I'm doing so. I think I must be robotic and everyone knows—metal legs, a metal heart. There is no thumping when the doctors search for a pulse. I try to say, *save your breath*, but my voice doesn't seem to work. They stare straight past me and on they go, walking through my torso as if I'm made of smoke. Maybe I'm not metal, but smoke? Or maybe I am both. Can someone be both? Everybody knows except me, so I try to ask who I am but my voice doesn't work.

I scream and no one even turns a head. I scream, I scream, *ice cream*? What was I talking about? My mind is deteriorating at a rapid pace and I can't seem to remember. Each blink and another memory is gone. Extraction. It's a new form of therapy. It's good at erasing all that dirty dark stuff, but there are some drawbacks. I can't remember what brushing my teeth looks like, why I don't have a pulse, how to drive a car, where to pay my bills. What is a toaster? A fridge? A shower? I don't know anything and no one talks to me. Lonely. I am so lonely.

10/17/18

I have a broken relationship with Hope—codependent and abusive in nature. We play one another like last week's song. We eat leftover lasagna from each other's mouths, chewing and spitting the noodles into one another's glazed eyes. Hope comes as he wishes, and leaves without warning. I tried to map the behavior once to find a pattern, to find any sort of precursor to his departure, but I found none. There was no way of knowing when I would be left standing on the doorstep holding that damn lasagna, begging him to please come back. But he leaves because Hope is deaf. He cannot make out my cries and he cannot read my lips. Hope can only smell my resistance. He knows when I don't want him around. He is special in that way. You can't lie to Hope.

I met Hope when I was a kid lying somewhere in my room—cold, alone, and covered in my own tears. He slithered right out of my mouth and onto my stomach. He grew and grew until he was big enough to hold me in his arms. He sang to me and kept me warm. He dried my tears and drowned out my cries with his voice. Hope was there when I felt abandoned. Therefore, I understand when he had to leave. He leaves when I am not ready and comes back when I need to be loved. Hope's love is not conditional. It is situational. He's like Batman, swooping in at the moment when all seems lost, warming a stark mind and breathing life into frozen lungs. He is a superhero, there when you think you won't survive.

Hope has been gone for many days now. My mind is growing apathetic, cynical, and weary. I feel the gray painting, the landscape in front of my eyes. My throat is sore, my head hurts, everyone makes me irritable, and suddenly those menacing thoughts are back...*no one wants*

you, you are unlovable, you are everyone's second choice, you are
nothing…nothing…nothing.

I lay in bed for two hours staring at the wall next to my bed.
I was tired. My whole body felt like lead and I couldn't
move. I didn't have any motivation to move. I closed my
eyes to be met with awful images. The crying little girl
slapped me in the face and awoke every ounce of fear left in
my bones. I should eat. I should eat. I should eat, but I know
I won't. I barely had the energy to blink, let alone make
myself dinner.

I fell asleep for an hour and reset my mind enough to put
two feet on the ground. I ate grapes and a cookie, which felt
sufficient enough for the night. I showered, mechanically
going through the motions while keeping the lights off.
Always keep the lights off. There's less chance of catching a
glimpse of my round body.

Hope never came back, which marks four days without him.
I've gone longer. I've endured worse, but I am tired of
enduring. I am tired of fighting. I guess that's why God
invented rest.

10/20/18

A year ago today, I overdosed. I filled my palm with a million white dots and prayed as the lethal snowflakes met the acid fire of my stomach.

I wanted to die. In fact, all I thought about this time last year was dying, and what the sweet release of endless darkness could offer me. The relapse into hopelessness was quick. Within sixteen days, I was systematically falling apart. My stomach brought up blood, my heart raced into my throat, and my intestines screamed. I was cold, exhausted, and incoherent. I had dropped X pounds. The demise was impressive, even by my standards.

This time last year solidified to me that mental illness is real. I had been doing so well. I discharged from a passionate and fulfilling treatment stay in May, feeling, for the first time, confident in my recovery. Then October 3rd rolled around, and all of a sudden, I couldn't get out of bed. I hit a wall, an invisible one. Certainly one I could not have planned for because I hadn't known it existed in the first place.

Everything was heavy again. Everything was bleak. I woke up and didn't want to be awake. From October 3rd of last year until the overdose, all I did was sleep, binge, purge, and dream of dying. It was the quickest and most sadistic fall I had ever experienced. It wasn't warranted. It was, by no means, welcomed. Yet, there I was—bulimic and fading. Mental illness is real, kids. It's so real, it scares me.

Twelve months have passed since kissing death. The first three were hell. I had to drag myself back to the land of the living through a cement tunnel by my own teeth, and worst of all, I didn't even want to. I wanted nothing to do with the living. I felt dead inside and outside, and everywhere life touched my exposed and vulnerable skin. I felt my time was up and yet my eyes were still opening, and my lungs continued to fill with air. I hated everyone who kept me alive. I hated the doctors and the nurses, counselors and my loved ones. I hated the medicine and the machines. I hated the sticky socks they made me wear to designate me as a fall risk. I was completely and utterly humiliated by my life, ashamed of the host I had become as I allowed the parasites in my brain to feed off my insecurities for so long, that there was none of me left. The weeks consisted of hospital visits and ambulance rides for a heart damaged over the years of abuse, forced meals into a body that only knew how to throw them back up, and therapy sessions where I had nothing left to say. The three months following the overdose were the hardest of my life.

Then New Year's Eve came along, and I came to the end of myself. I stood on a ledge the eating disorder had built with a thorny forest behind my back and nothing in front. Then, somehow I mustered enough courage to leap straight off that cliff toward emptiness—an unwritten story, a mysterious landscape. New Year's Eve, I checked myself out of treatment, got a tattoo, watched the ball drop, and made a promise to myself to never look back. The chapter of illness and hospital gowns, of ambulances and IV's, was all over. This year was mine. I had earned some peace of mind.

They say you can't will yourself out of mental illness, but I only think that's half true. I think you need support and resources in the beginning stages of recovery, but I believe that eventually you come to a tipping point. All the years of struggling filled your pot full of shit, and recovery comes the moment you receive the inner willingness and desire to tip it over. Once the shit is spilled, it can't go back in. It's like spilling a glass of milk—you can't collect the fluid back into the glass. Every person who has reached recovery has had a tipping moment, the moment when they knew it wasn't worth it anymore—where they were so fed up with the disease that they would do anything in their power to beat it.

I stood in the treatment center that New Year's Eve and looked around at the curled up grown women underneath blankets and feeding tubes and walked out. I grab my things and left AMA. I don't know where it came from, but I just knew—I knew this was not where I needed to be anymore. And, it was the best decision I've made for myself.

Months three through twelve have been transforming. I have never had such a long winning streak. Life keeps amazing me. Opportunities keep falling into my lap, and over and over again I am met with the reality that life can be good. It can taste sweet and feel safe and offer hope. Life is not the thorny forest, but the clouds I met through my leap of faith. I don't know what lies at the bottom, but it is better that way. If I knew, there'd be no excitement in the journey. I have grown to enjoy life's surprises. I am learning to expect good and gracious gifts, where previously I believed the world could only offer me demons. I have grasped opportunities this year that I never thought were possible.

Going to Thailand, training to be a yoga teacher, dating Erik, camping in Costa Rica, the road trip through Florida, diving in caves, establishing UJ as a business, making a calendar, commissioning art, reading, flying, eating, and drinking. I learned how to be completely and unapologetically myself.

It's been a whirlwind of catching up. There's so much life to take in, and I feel like I have I a lot of ground to make up.

These days I experience life on acid, because I never had life pouring into me before. It's all colorful and trippy, euphoric and terrifying. Life is a friend and an idol. Life is my lifelong guardian. I've had so many near misses, but here's to twelve months of breathing and many more to come.

10/23/18

i dance across cliffs tickling clouds
kiss sharks through un-clenched teeth
and hold fire between my bare palms
my spirit is wild and unapologetic
it dances without a concept of fear

i've known a thousand lifetimes
because my body kept the score
through tally marks lining my legs
and mountain ridges rising and falling
to form ribs protecting a frozen heart

through past lives i learned the trick
of swallowing abusive fire
knowing one day the explosion
would take thieves with me
then from the ashes i'd rise

a child
with hands that burned as flames
so that everyone i touched
remembered
for once
they remembered my name

10/29/18

Everything is different moment by moment. Things peak and then crash each time I open my mouth to breathe. My lungs are unstable pipe bombs that vacillate between filling with fire or cotton, leaving me to either breathe out sparks or clouds. Waking up usually begins with a neutral emotional radar, one in which there is no attachment to how the day is going to pan out. But, then somewhere along the passing moments, I feel my thighs rub together or my stomach crinkle into a cascade of rolls. Something, anything—a memory, a song, a smell—could set off the pipe bombs of my lungs. Then I breathe out fire and heat and rage and despair. Internally I spiral, slowly unwinding everything that was true moments before. Everything becomes bleak and hopeless, and relapse feels like my only option. I become flooded with memories and past mistakes. I am haunted by the voices of past selves whispering of my worthlessness and failures. Essentially I explode—my lungs pop, ricocheting debris and destruction through my throat and out my mouth. Through my eyes, the entire room crumbles as I melt, and everyone around sees this dramatic decline, but, in reality, it's invisible. The whole explosion that is causing my complete emotional breakdown, only I can see. I am alone. Completely alone in a war that no one knows anything about, and that is worse than swallowing your own bombs.

I could open my mouth and tell those who love me when I am at war. I could explain to them what it feels like—how I am truly doing, what is going on inside my brain—but that feels like betrayal. Betrayal of my mind, my recovery, and most importantly their trust, because bombs go off all the time. I don't know when the bombs will be triggered. I can't predict why, who, or what will cause the warfare. Fear keeps me from believing that loved ones won't be overly worried when they discover how violent my internal experience can still be. I believe that they believe that things are now calm, neutral, and stable—which they are in comparison to where I have come from. I have moved from the front lines to an army base that is targeted regularly, but not under an immediate death threat.

But the reality of recovery from any addiction is that it is a constant battle, and I'm not sure that anyone who has not walked through the struggle could understand how it's not always hopeless. Those of us in recovery know that it's not always bleak and dark, but how can you explain that war isn't always terrible? That there are moments of joy, freedom, love, community, confidence, and hope? Even soldiers find a family away from home. They eat meals together. They find joy in the sunshine. There is a sense of accomplishment when they go to bed at night because, hey, they lived. They survived another day. Addicts, when we lie down sober from our addictive behaviors, feel the same. We lived. We lived another day without destroying ourselves.

As the months pass and I get farther into recovery, I start to forget I am at war. I believe that one day, the war will come to an end, that true freedom comes when my flag is planted into the ground and all my demons retreat. I kill more with each passing day. I become stronger. My enemies grow more fearful. The war has been going on for so long, but I am finally on the winning side. Some demons are even converting and beginning to fight on my behalf. Even they are tired. We all just want some peace. And, I believe you innately begin to manifest the things you desire most.

Peace comes in the form of car rides with the windows down and the music up loud. Joy sparks when Erik and I dance through the streets at night in the rain, critiquing societal standards simply by being alive. Freedom comes during midnight custard runs or pie parties with my roommates. The brick wall that kept me from life is breaking down, and I am getting more and more tastes of the other side. This is why the moments where my lungs explode and fall deeply into myself through a battle of fury and rage are bearable. I take them with stride. I welcome them in the same way I have learned to greet rejection.

One more battle with my mind brings me one step closer to total freedom in recovery.

11/19/18

Nothing feels right because it is all allusive and cloudy. I'm wrapped in cellophane, witnessing the world through a plastic sheet, but it's okay because I don't need air to breathe. I learned long ago to survive through my own mind. I can create oxygen by merely dreaming of it. My lungs will fill and deflate. I'll never collapse because I am the maker of my own life source. My mind is a place of solace when the thunder begins to roar and the lightning strikes and the war outside becomes as real as the rain crashing onto my plastic skin. I create things, whole worlds inside my head that never existed. They never will exist, at least not in this world. They are too precious to be given to thieves and fools to witness. These worlds are mine. I only allow pieces of them to leak out through color, through words, through my tangible creations, which this world calls art. My mind is stormy and turbulent. It can be lonely and terrifying and magical all at one time. It has rivers, valleys, and oceans to be explored. I have no fear of the depths of the crevices. I only have fear of how the depths will be carved into reality. If I slip too far down inside this mind of mine, I may never come back up. Deep into the ocean trenches marks uncharted territories, which even I cannot predict what lies below. Monsters and creatures of the night lie waiting to be destroyed. How can one know themselves if they do not conquer their mind?

The monsters reveal themselves in glimpses. I still feel their hands around my throat and forget that I have the power to create my own oxygen. I choke. Words won't leave my lips—I can't breathe—but then I snap back. I am fine. I have always been fine.

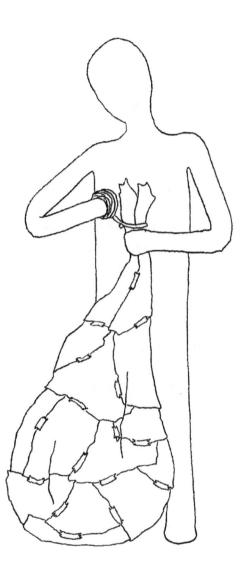

2019: *learning to live in a space where years aren't dictated by relapses and treatment stays, but carved through the passing days of simply living*

01/11/19

Sometimes life takes you in its grip, twirls you around, and leaves you dazed and confused about what day, time, or month you are living in. I haven't written consistently in two months or so, and I feel this intense loosening of my spirit. Disconnection has become a consistent friend. My legs feel as if they are walking on air, not quite grounded to the floor beneath my feet. It's not dissociation—I tell my therapist this over and over. I know dissociation. It comes and goes like the rising and falling of the waves. I will not deny tasting its sweet numbness once or twice over the last month, but this disconnection is different. I am not disconnected from life. I am disconnected from the passage of time. Rather than checking out from my emotional experiences or denying myself the space to truly experience life, I am totally and completely in it. Each day is a day. Not a battle, not a struggle, but a day. I haven't fantasized about relapses, obsessively planned out my meals, or found ways to sabotage the good things in my life.

"I am fine," I told my therapist.

"What do you mean by fine?" she asked.

"I finally feel like a normal person," I answered.

Normalcy and stability are foreign concepts to me, so I assumed a position of operating in a constant state of crisis. I lived off the rocky grounds in which mental illness forced me to walk. Running away from problems and numbing the positive experiences in my life became habitual—a reflex of sorts, my default or guide on how to deal with life. I lacked the capacity to hold any sort of emotion. It was too unpredictable. It threatened my semblance of control.

Therefore, to have months where I float from one day to the next, not threatened or fazed by the experiences at hand, feels strange. The reality is that within these last two months, I haven't paused to question this new state of being. I was consumed in living. Between dating, dinners, parties, trips, work, art-making, and so much more…my time was filled. Who was I to stop to question the way things were unfolding?

The New Year gives us the space for reflection. We are bombarded with New Year's resolutions, diet and weight loss goals, as well as endless ways which people claim they are going to improve themselves. Since finding recovery, I have taken the approach of setting intentions for the New Year, rather than goals. As part of my healing process, I have learned to challenge these beliefs that I am not okay where I am right now, that I need to improve or better myself in certain ways. Intentions seem to offer a much more compassionate approach to the New Year. For 2019, I have chosen the word JOY to meditate on. I have chosen JOY as a direct reaction to these last two months of life. As I find more and more freedom within my days to simply be, so too, does my level of joyousness increase. I want to lean into this carefree spirit that I was naturally born with so that I may continue to invite JOY into my days.

Now, I don't want to bullshit anyone—not everything has been rainbows and sunshine. Every day has ups and downs—let's be real, there is no high without the occasional low. 2019 began with a cop pulling me over at 12:30 a.m. Not even thirty minutes into the New Year, and I was already having to challenge my negative emotions and remind myself of my intention I had set not even an hour earlier.

"It's a bad omen," I said through tears the rest of the way home.

"It's a personal challenge," Erik told me.

Life is funny that way, challenging you, giving you constant opportunities to strengthen your personal ability to succeed. Here we are now a week into the New Year, and my living environment has gone from neutral to hostile. One roommate has decided that screaming battles, passive aggressive actions such as slamming a loud vacuum against my door while I am sleeping, and mocking me on speaker phone are appropriate reactions to a simple confrontation about needing her to help out with the cleaning schedule. At this point, all I can do is laugh—hopefully with the universe—at how blatantly opposing these situations are to my intention of JOY. How am I supposed to find JOY in the midst of fights and traffic tickets? The answer I have come up with is this—by being grateful that I am far enough into my recovery to handle these situations without my eating disorder. Right now, this answer is more than enough for me.

02/06/19

My workspace today was a café carved out of a rocky hill overlooking the crystal clear ocean, which was lined with longboats and palm trees. The café was warm, but between my coffee frappe and the sea breeze I was comfortable. My stomach was full of smoothies, french fries, club sandwiches, and contentment. About two weeks ago, I ran off to a remote island off the coast of Thailand called Koh Phangan. I spent a large portion of last summer on this same island, and ever since its energy has not let me go. The crystal ocean waves wake me up in the morning and the sounds of birds sing me to sleep in the evening. My days are filled with yoga, waterfall hiking, scuba diving, and an endless amount of Thai food. I look out from this café, pausing my work for a moment, to reflect on how blessed I am.

2018, I named my year. It was the year of recovery, the year of pulling myself out of darkness, and walking into the light. It was the year of new beginnings, new mindsets, and a new way of experiencing the world. 2018, by all means, ended up being my year. I spent it healthy, joyful, and open to new opportunities. When 2019 rolled around, I reflected on what intention I wanted to set for the upcoming months. I thought about my life and felt at peace. I had no idea where the future was going to take me. I had no direct career path, little money, and only a year of recovery under my belt—yet there wasn't any anxiety. So, I chose to name 2019 the year of joy. This year I intend to truly slow down and experience life in all its glory.

The first month of the year has passed. February has begun and with it, I feel a rush of accomplishment. I'm at a café on my favorite island, editing underwater pictures for a dive shop. The jobs I hold let me do what I love—diving and yoga—while living in a place that awakens every spark of joy within me.

It is never easy to get on a plane and jet-off halfway across the world. I've done it several times now, but never like this. I never left without knowing where I was going next. I never left with a future that was so uncertain or a career that wasn't set in stone. People consider me a free spirit, but my freedom usually comes with conditions. I wanted a return date on my plane ticket, and I want to have a five-year plan for success in my back pocket. I am teaching at the same two hundred-hour TTC that I trained with last year. This week we talked about the Yamas of yogic philosophy. I felt struck by the Yama of non-attachment. Why is it that I feel so attached to a plan? Why is it that in order to feel successful I need to have a steady income, hold a five year plan, and currently be in grad school or better yet, working on my doctorate?

Growing up in the U.S., I was blessed with an enormous amount of privilege. I think about this each time I wash my dishes outside, fill up my motorbike with gas out of a glass bottle, or lug huge water bottles back to my bungalow because the faucet water isn't safe. But, what some fail to notice is that with privilege comes expectations. Somewhere over the last century, the American Dream has morphed from chasing possibilities to holding societal expectations. The American Dream has turned into graduating high school with a 4.0, going to a four-year college, going to graduate school, possibly going on to get a doctorate, getting married, having a full-time job, having kids, buying a house, shopping at Whole Foods, going to Core Power, and eating acai bowls.

By no means have I led a traditional path, and I have no intention to. I find a future that is predictable and etched through society's ideals depressing and dull. Editing photos while sipping on coffee, listening to the waves, and soaking up all the sun's vitamins, sounds much more alluring.

Therefore, whenever I question the future—whenever the anxieties of the unknowns come into play, or worries about money, success, and image plagued my thoughts—all I have to do is look out my window. I look out and see courage. I feel sand, see the palm trees, and hear the jungle and ocean. I see an island that is thousands of miles from my comfort zone, but makes me feel right at home. I see the leap of faith I took in 2019, into completely unknown territory. I see all this and I feel joy—the exact emotion I intended to fill this year with. Now, it's only been a month, but I'd say that we are well on our way to a joy filled year.

02/09/19

I'm thirteen hours ahead of everyone back home. Saturday is ending here, while the sun just came up in Chicago. Time is a warped concept that leaves me feeling upside down and backwards, never quite knowing what to make of its strange and twisted factors. The half-moon is in three days. The tides are slowly receding with the moon's magnetic pull. More and more of the sandy beach becomes exposed each evening as I walk – toes shifting, hands swatting mosquitoes – back to my bungalow. The moon sits high above me, in outer-space—along with all the stars above my head. There's Leo and Capricorn and Cancer, and even my Scorpio shining high above me. I'm so small and the world is so big, and time is even bigger, and I can't help but get lost in the complexities of all that is around me.

Then I walk inside. I open the door to the bungalow, turn on the fan, and grab my towel to shower. My mind switches from the wonder of the stars and moon to the worries of critique and judgment. I have teaching-fright big time here on the island. I stay up for hours before I teach a yoga class, worrying and obsessing over everything I could do wrong. I meditate and do my best to calm my mind, but then somehow my dreams turn back toward the anxieties that await with the sunrise. Even my subconscious gives me little rest. I sent over photographs and a video to the boss of the dive shop I am working with, feeling inadequate with each file I uploaded, doubting my abilities, doubting my projects. If I didn't receive jaw-dropping amazement as feedback, I wrote everything else off as a failure. Black and white, anxious and self-deprecating—this was my dark side.

Then I walk inside. I open the door to the bungalow, turn on the fan, and grab my towel to shower. I make jokes through the door with my partner and listen to the faint rustle of the waves in the distance. My thoughts are preoccupied but my soul is at ease. My body is content, browned, and freckled by the intense Thailand sun. My knees and hips are scraped from the playful waterfalls I have climbed, the rocks I have slipped on, and the current I fell down. The very tip of my nose is red from a tropical kiss too harsh, and my feet are worn and blistered from my stubbornness to never drive a motorbike. My body is content. My body is home here. The stars stay in my soul, flickering deep within as I shave one calf and then the other. Scorpio's nature pulses through my bones and the fading moon phases fascinate my spirit. My soul is at home here—this is my light side.

I carry around two selves. My mental illness is a part of me and I believe it always will be. I can't turn back time and rewrite the past. I take the past, kiss it on the forehead, then put it in my back pocket and move forward with my life. My eating disorder used to be larger than my light side. It used to be a monster that controlled everything I did. There was no room to hear what the soul or body had to say because the mind was constantly running the show. But, over the years I have learned how to starve the beast—how to ignore its presence and begin to move on with my life. Time passed and the monster grew smaller and smaller until it was small enough for me to pluck it off the ground and shove into my back pocket. I have two selves, but one is much smaller than the other. The dark side, this small self, sits in my back pocket. Every once in a while the monster will poke me in the butt, reminding me of my insecurities as an artist, yoga teacher, or simply as a human being. Every once in a while, the dark side will follow me into the shower and ransack my brain while my body and soul are deeply connected with the earth around.

This complex order of things, the two selves, the diminishing of the dark and its periodic resurrection, reminds me of time. It reminds me of my inability to understand the layers, the concept, the complex order of things. As human beings we are complicated creatures. We have so many depths to our nature. It is arrogant to believe I will ever figure them all out. So for tonight, I am content with recognizing that my mind is busy flirting with darkness while my body and soul are thriving in the light— such is the duality of life, the dialectic of the entire universe we live in.

02/27/19

Eating Disorder Awareness Week

I didn't know eating disorder awareness week existed until I went to treatment. Treatment changed me, opened me up to ideas, movements, advocacy, and hope. It showed me the army of people fighting on the other side of this disease, which is an illness I convinced myself for many years I didn't have. This week gives me, as well as all those who have struggled or know someone who has struggled with an eating disorder, the opportunity to share our stories. If there is anything I have learned in my fight for recovery, it's that sharing my story is my greatest weapon against darkness, because it gives me the opportunity to connect. With connection comes community, and with community comes healing.

This eating disorder awareness week, I am writing my first post on a beach in Cambodia. I am on a remote island off the southern coast that doesn't have roads, ATMs, or modern conveniences Westerners are used to—like hot water or toilet paper. Last night I was reading a memoir about all the pain the Cambodian people have endured from the genocide that ravaged the country in the 1970-'80s, when suddenly I got sick, like really sick. I was on the floor shaking, cold, clammy, with a twisting stomach. I blamed it on the water, yellow with rust that I brushed my teeth in earlier, but part of me wondered if the sickness was not brought on by empathy. Empathy and heartbreak for a people so broken, hurt, and traumatized. I look out at the beautiful crystal clear waters and can hardly conceptualize the juxtaposition between the beauty and the horror of the people—it makes me sick.

I feel the same way when I think about mental illness. In using Thailand's slogan – the country I spent time in previous to moving to Cambodia – the two are *same, same, but different*. I don't know genocide. I don't know war. I don't know outward inflicted starvation. I do, however, know epidemics. I do know internal war. I know self-inflicted starvation. People all over the world experience hardships that tear them down and bring them toward the brink of all they know.

Nevertheless, it's eating disorder awareness week and I feel obligated to reflect on my own journey, but this year I don't exactly want to. Instead, I want to reflect on recovery. Recovery is not following a meal plan to a tee, or exercising the exact amount allotted to you by a dietitian. It is not eating one slice of cake on your birthday, or adding cream one time to your coffee. These are all positive steps because they lead us in the right direction. But, at the end of the day this isn't recovery. I feel as if I have the right to say this because I used to believe these actions equaled recovery. Maybe they do for some, but I have come to uncover a whole different meaning of the word.

On New Year's Eve of 2017 (going on a year and a half now), I made a choice for 2018. I drove myself home to Chicago, all alone in a car, confused and heartbroken, but determined to never allow my eating disorder to overtake my life again. 2018 was going to be my year. Now, I have had moments of recovery epiphanies where I am elated at the idea of getting better and moving forward toward health, but this was different. This was a tired, beat, and surrendering moment. It was a lone decision, a quiet determination made by a very emotionally stricken girl. Yet, here I am over a year later, and I can say with confidence that my eating disorder was not a part of the last year and two months. There were hard days, but never more than that. Emotions were tumultuous and I was sad and confused at the beginning, but recovery was what I decided to achieve, so recovery was where I was headed.

Generally people who have eating disorders are incredibly intelligent and determined. We are stubborn, strong-willed, detail-oriented, and fiercely compassionate. All of these traits, when channeled in the right direction, can powerfully propel us toward complete liberation—if we are only to switch the goal from shrinking to freedom.

In the past year I have accomplished little in society's eyes, but that's not the point. The point is how much I have accomplished internally—how much happiness and freedom I have been able to channel. As I think back on all my adventures of scuba diving, yoga teacher training, country hopping, dating, falling in love, and eating good food, I'd say that I have found freedom. I have reached a point that I never dreamed was possible.

05/18/19

Everything points towards the basics, like counting to ten and naming the colors. My mind recoils at the sound of loneliness and spits out an eleven-year-old girl untethered to this world, a girl lost and confused and completely abandoned while simultaneously being surrounded by dozens of people. My mind splits and throws into my face the child I never wished to be, the story stolen, the black holes, and blurry landscapes. *I don't even know who I am anymore*, I whisper to no one. The room is an empty hole which I fell into around 9:00 p.m. and now I'm afraid I may never find my way back out. *You are okay, okay, okay...* my words fall away, echoing into the silence of the apartment and I realize that no sound ever left my lips. No matter how badly I want to, I can't scream out, but I don't mind because I don't want anyone to see these parts. The times when my mind escapes me and leaves me paralyzed in a moment frozen in my past, believing that if I were only to thaw the pain, then perhaps I could stop coming back. But it doesn't work that way because when that pain is thawed, another one comes and another and another until there's an entire traffic jam lined up and I become a gapers' delay for future therapists to line up and gawk at. An animal on display with a fascinating and complex story to tell. It's layered, it's dark, it's painful, it's called trauma, and instead of pulling it apart piece by piece and leaving me as a patchwork quilt lying mute in the dark, I'd rather just return to the basics. I'd rather name my colors and draw a fucking bunny because at least then I am not part of the quilt work, and instead I am a human sitting with a person who wants to listen and not gawk, to hear without words, to feel without tears. At least the crayons on the paper can give voice to the words never allowed to leave my lips. It's in the shaking foot and absent eyes that the person knows to stop, to draw, to pull me away from the ice and back into an office in downtown Chicago where I get to sit and share my story with as few words as I deem necessary.

I never want to leave. I never want to walk out of that room on the third floor with the upside down painting because when I do, that means it's closer to the end, the end of the drawings, the end of the colors, and stories, the end of the silence creating words. It's the end of something that has helped my abandoned child feel less of the enemy and a little more like an injured friend. I don't know why God wants me to leave, to move across the country, and leave behind the room. But they asked me to, and so I'm going because God has never steered me wrong in the past. Trust is not something I learned. It's something I taught myself. I fought to find the foundation on which I built my future life. I knelt on hands and knees alone in Chicago at eighteen laying brick by brick for this room I can now find healing in. It all leads somewhere. All the blood and sweat and tears, all the hospitals and treatments centers, the therapists, the meals— it wasn't for nothing. I will never believe it was for nothing because if it was, then I wouldn't be visited by a lonely eleven-year-old girl. I would still be that child because none of my story would have changed. I changed because I built this fucking house. The scars on my thighs are a testament to the resiliency I hold within this chest. I have experienced things that would make people crumble at their mere mention. I became strong because strong was the only thing I could become. Because the sun still rose and the days went on and somehow I had to get my ass out of bed and continue. I endured it. I took each blow as a lesson on how to dodge the next one. My life was a training, a preparation to launch me into a world I know nothing about but everything it isn't. I know the underside and for once, I have the choice to dig myself through to the surface. And so here

I am, twenty-four, and I choose to start with numbers, colors, bunnies, and notes because all the basics will lead me to a destination I can't even fathom.

I will make it, I whisper to the dark, and this time I feel a faint brush of air signaling the turning of this chapter, the beginning of the next page in my forever changing book.

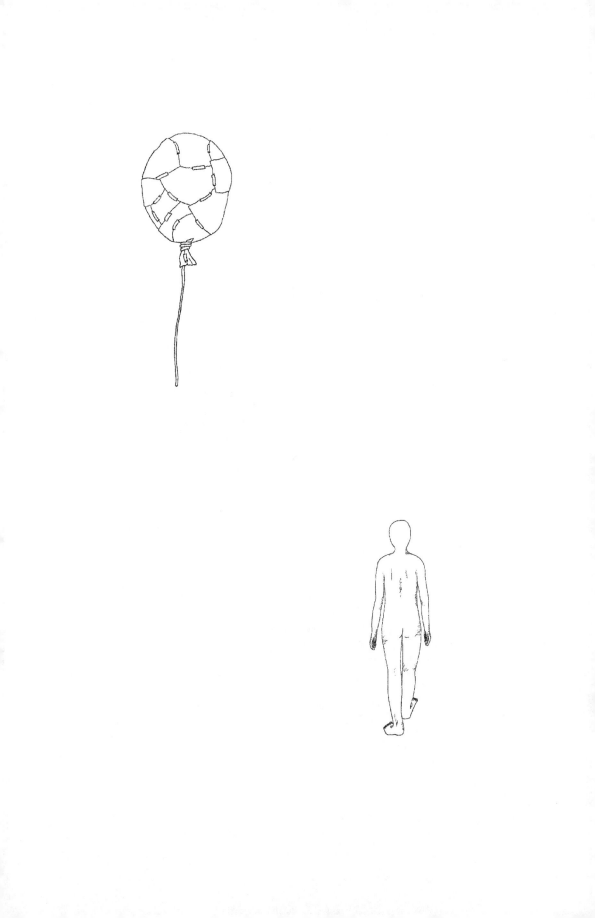

CPSIA information can be obtained
at www.ICGtesting.com
Printed in the USA
LVHW102201011219
639097LV00009B/704/P

9 781949 351873